Contemporary Theory Workbook

book 1

by Margaret Brandman

Exclusive Distributors for Australia and New Zealand
Encore Music Distributors 227 Napier St, Fitzroy. 3065 Victoria. Australia
Ph +61 3 9415 6677 Facsimile +61 3 9415 6655
Email: sales@encoremusic.com.au

This book © Copyright 2009 by Margaret Brandman trading as Jazzem Music
46 Gerrale St, Cronulla NSW 2230 Australia
ISBN 978-0-949683-43-4
Order No. MMP 8067
International Copyright Secured (APRA/AMCOS) All Rights Reserved

Unauthorised reproduction of any part of this publication by any means
including photocopying, is an infringement of copyright.

Contents - Part A

Introduction 4
Lesson 1   Staff or Stave, Line Notes and Space Notes 5
Lesson 2   Leger Lines, Low and High sounds 6
Lesson 3   Intervals: Prime (Same), Second (Step) and Third (Skip) 7
Lesson 4   Interval Exercises 8
Lesson 5   More Intervals: Fourth (Skip-Plus-One) and Fifth (Jump) 9
Lesson 6   More Interval Exercises 10
Lesson 7   Bar Lines, Interval Exercises 11
Lesson 8   Note names, the keyboard 12
Lesson 9   Clefs: Treble Clef (G Clef), Bass Clef (F Clef) and C Clef 13
Lesson 10   Writing Practice - Clefs and Braces 14
Lesson 11   The Treble Clef - Signpost Cs and note-names 15
Lesson 12   The Bass Clef - Signpost Cs and note-names 16
Lesson 13   C Clefs - Alto and Tenor - Signpost Cs and note-names 17
Lesson 14   The Great Staff - Signpost Cs and note-names 18
Lesson 15   More note-naming on the Great Staff and in C Clef 19
Lesson 16   Notes and Rests 20
Lesson 17   Writing Practice - Notes and Rests 21
Lesson 18   Time Values 22
Lesson 19   Dotted Notes and Dotted Rests 23
Lesson 20   The Time-Signature 24
Lesson 21   Simple Time; 2/4, 3/4, 4/4 25
Lesson 22   More on Timing and Counting 26
Lesson 23   Grouping of Notes and Rests 27
Lesson 24   Fill in the missing Notes and Rests 28
Lesson 25   Stems and Beams 29
Lesson 26   Whole Tones and Semitones. Sharp, Flat and Natural 30
Lesson 27   Sharps 31
Lesson 28   Flats 32
Lesson 29   More on Sharps and Flats 33
Lesson 30   More on Semitones and Whole Tones 34
Lesson 31   The Major Scale. Key Signature 35
Lesson 32   More on Key Signatures. Scale writing 36
Lesson 33   The Natural Sign. Accidentals 37
Lesson 34   Exercises on Accidentals 38
Lesson 35   Test Your Knowledge 39
Answer Sheet 40

Contents - Part B

Lesson 1	Larger Intervals: Sixth, Seventh and Octave	42
Lesson 2	Harmonic and Melodic Intervals; Interval Families	43
Lesson 3	Note-naming on the Grand Staff. Two new Cs	44
Lesson 4	Musical Terms indicating Volume	45
Lesson 5	Degree Numbers and Degree Names	46
Lesson 6	Key Signature Patterns - Sharp Keys	47
Lesson 7	Key Signature Patterns - Flat Keys	48
Lesson 8	Major Scales; Scale Pattern and the Tetrachord	49
Lesson 9	Major Scales - Sharp Keys	50
Lesson 10	Remaining Major Scales - Sharp Keys	51
Lesson 11	Major Scales - Flat Keys	52
Lesson 12	Remaining Major Scales - Flat Keys	53
Lesson 13	The Circle or Cycle of Fifths	54
Lesson 14	Note Naming in Soprano, Mezzo-Soprano and Baritone Clef	55
Lesson 15	Musical Terms indicating Tempo or Pace	56
Lesson 16	Sixteenth Notes or Semiquavers	57
Lesson 17	Exercises on Sixteenth Notes	58
Lesson 18	The Chromatic Scale	59
Lesson 19	More Simple Meter Time-Signatures	60
Lesson 20	Group A Time Signatures; 2/2, 3/2, 4/2	61
Lesson 21	More on Group A time Signatures	62
Lesson 22	Group B Time Signatures; 2/8, 3/8, 4/8	63
Lesson 23	Ties and Slurs	64
Lesson 24	More Musical Terms, Signs and Symbols	65
Lesson 25	Major and Minor Thirds	66
Lesson 26	The Major Triad	67
Lesson 27	The Minor Triad	68
Lesson 28	The Diminished Triad	69
Lesson 29	The Augmented Triad	70
Lesson 30	The Suspended Fourth Triad	71
Lesson 31	Major and Minor Chords in Inversions	72
Lesson 32	Exercises on Inversions; Diminished & Augmented Chords in Inversions	73
Lesson 33	Suspended Fourth Triads in Inversions	74
Lesson 34	Repeat Signs: Double Dots; 1st and 2nd Endings	75
Lesson 35	Exercises on Repeat Signs	76
Lesson 36	Repeat Signs: 3rd Endings	77
Lesson 37	Test Your Knowledge	78
Answer Sheet		79

Introduction

This book is part of my 'Contemporary' series of books and ear-training materials. The materials in these series provide an holistic view of music, dealing with the **practical, theoretical and aural aspects of music**.

Taking a practical and common-sense approach, the Contemporary Theory Workbooks provide students with an overview of many aspects of music theory, revealing many musical mysteries which traditional theory books have neglected in the past. The information presented allows the student to venture into popular, jazz and contemporary idioms as well as providing a solid foundation in the music of the western classical tradition. The page-per-lesson format encourages the student to see the whole picture (gestalt) of each topic, thereby reducing the time taken to learn the information.

There is an emphasis on the **interval approach** to assist with the comprehension of many concepts and to foster music speed-reading and learning in any clef.

Scales are approached from both the notational and keyboard pattern points of view, while the **cycle of fifths** and **all types of triads** are learned quite early in the series. These tools are invaluable for the improvising musician as well as the reader.

To simplify the topic of rhythm and duration, spatial diagrams have been presented. By colouring them in using the colour system presented in Book 2A of the Contemporary Piano Method, students will be able to fully understand the duration of the notes via the accelerated learning tools of touch, spatial orientation and colour.

Use of colour as a memory aid, will promote the understanding of **time signatures**, and help with other topics such as interval families and chord construction.

The colours for note-values are as follows –

- Double whole note/ breve ....mauve
- Whole note/semibreve ....purple
- Half note/ minim ....yellow
- Quarter note/crotchet ....blue
- Eighth note/ quaver ....red
- Sixteenth note/semiquaver ....green
- Thirty-second note/ demisemiquaver ....brown

Other materials to use alongside this book:

1. *Contemporary Theory Primer (CTP)* – focusing on interval patterns and rhythm boxes to be coloured and clapped
2. *Contemporary Chord Workbook – Book 1*. Best completed in tandem with the contemporary theory workbooks
3. *Contemporary Aural Course* – Preparatory for beginners and then Set One onwards
   Helping students understand the sounds and language of music, through listening, singing and transcription
4. *Contemporary Piano Method* – Junior Primer, Book 1A and Book 1B
5. *Playing Made Easy for Recorder* – Method Book and Tune Book (Australian editions)
6. *How to Play the Recorder* – American edition (Santorella Music)

I trust you will find this series and enjoyable and engaging way of learning about the sounds and language of music.

Margaret Brandman
Ph.D.(Mus/Arts), B.Mus (Syd)., T.Mus.A.,
F.Mus.Ed.ASMC., F.Comp.ASMC., L.Perf.ASMC., Hon.FNMSM., ASA T.Dip

International Woman of the Year for Music (2003)

LESSON ONE

THE STAFF OR STAVE

The STAFF or Stave is the set of FIVE LINES and FOUR SPACES on which music is written.

THE STAFF

The lines and spaces are numbered from bottom to top.

A note can be written on a LINE, in which case the line goes through the middle of the note, OR a note can be written in a SPACE in which case the note has a line either side of it.

LINE NOTE:　　　　　　　　　**SPACE NOTE:**

ALSO: Space Notes can be written on the top of the Fifth line or underneath the first line.

FOR EXAMPLE:

Music is written and read from Left to Right just as text is.

◆◆◆◆◆◆◆◆◆◆◆◆◆◆◆◆◆◆◆◆◆◆◆◆◆◆◆◆◆◆

EXERCISES

(1) Copy these notes on the staff.

(2) Indicate whether the following notes are Line Notes or Space Notes. Use L for Line and S for Space.

....

(3) Draw some **Line** Notes on the staff below.

(4) Draw some **Space** Notes on the staff below.

LESSON TWO

LEGER LINES

Leger lines are the small lines (Light lines *from the French word 'leger' meaning light*) written above or below the staff. They are used to extend the range of notes beyond limitations of the staff.

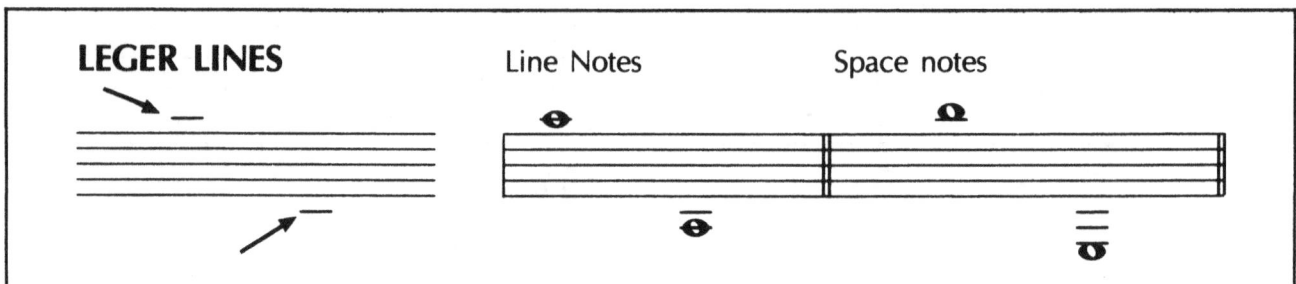

SOUNDS

If a note is written low on the Staff it will sound LOW.

If a note is written high on the Staff it will sound HIGH.

If a note is written on the same position on the Staff as the previous note, it will sound the SAME.

◆◆◆◆◆◆◆◆◆◆◆◆◆◆◆◆◆◆◆◆◆◆◆◆◆◆◆◆◆◆

EXERCISES

(1) Tick the HIGHEST note of each group.

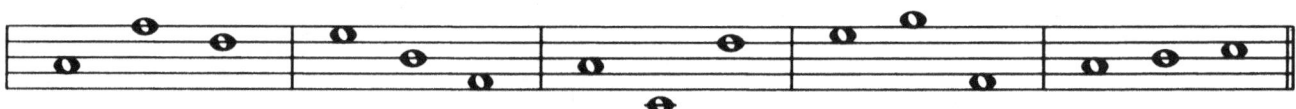

(2) Tick the LOWEST note of each group.

(3) Indicate whether the second note of each pair is higher, lower or the same as the first note.

....

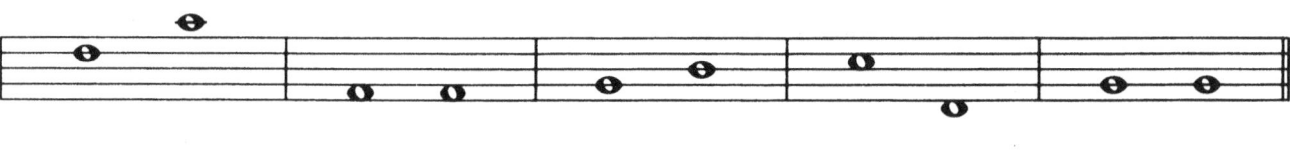

....

6

LESSON THREE

INTERVALS

Musical sounds are created when a series of notes are played or sung. The essence of a musical statement is the interval between any two notes. One note on its own cannot suggest a tune yet even two notes following each other can already present the germ of a musical idea.

SAME — If notes are repeated immediately following one another they are said to be moving the distance of a SAME or PRIME. If the two notes are played by different instruments at the same time they are said to be sounding in UNISON. *(Uni=same son=sound)*.

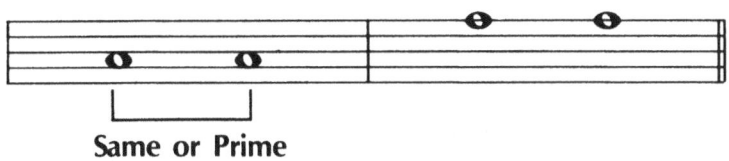

Same or Prime

STEP — When notes move up or down the staff using alternate lines and spaces, a ladder of notes can be seen. Notes moving along the ladder are said to be moving in STEPS or SECONDS.

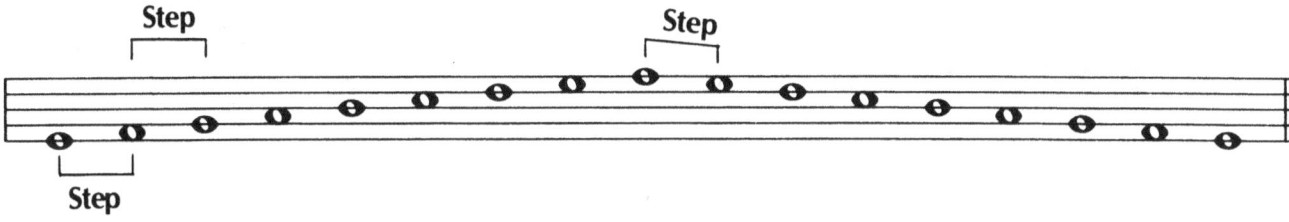

Steps or Seconds moving UP.   Steps or Seconds moving DOWN.

SKIP — When notes move up or down the staff, from one line to the next line, or from one space to the next space, skipping over one of the notes in the ladder, the interval between the two notes is known as a SKIP or THIRD.

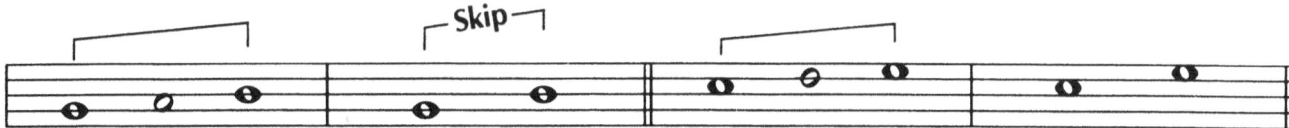

Skips or **Thirds** moving UP.

Skips or **Thirds** moving DOWN.

LESSON FOUR

INTERVAL EXERCISES

(1) Write repeated notes (SAMES) next to the given notes.

e.g.   S

(2) Write STEPS (Seconds) moving UP from the given notes.

e.g.   St↑

(3) Write STEPS moving DOWN from the given notes.

e.g.   St↓

(4) Write SKIPS (Thirds) moving either UP or DOWN from the given notes as indicated by the arrow.

e.g. Sk↑   Sk↓   Sk↑   Sk↑   Sk↓   Sk↓

Sk↑   Sk↓   Sk↓   Sk↑   Sk↑   Sk↓

(5) Indicate whether the following notes are moving by intervals of a SAME (Prime), STEP (Second) or SKIP (Third). Also show the direction the notes are moving by using arrows like this:

↑ UP.,   ↓ DOWN.

Write **S** for a **Same**, **St** for a **Step** and **Sk** for a **Skip**.

e.g. St↑   Sk↓

LESSON FIVE

MORE INTERVALS

SKIP-PLUS-ONE — The next size of interval after the Skip or Third, is the SKIP-PLUS-ONE or FOURTH. The notes which form this interval are always written from a Line Note to a Space Note or vice-versa. The gap between these notes is further than in the distance of a Step which is also written from Line Note to Space Note.

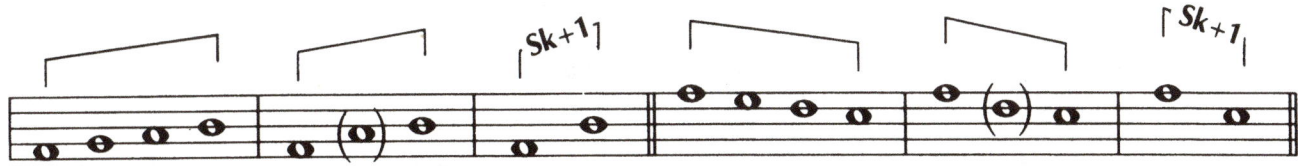

Skip-Plus-One or Fourth
moving UP

Skip-Plus-One or Fourth
moving DOWN

JUMP — The JUMP or FIFTH is the next size of interval after the Skip-Plus-One or Fourth. The notes in the interval of a JUMP always move from Line to Line or from Space to Space, while jumping over one line or space as the case may be.

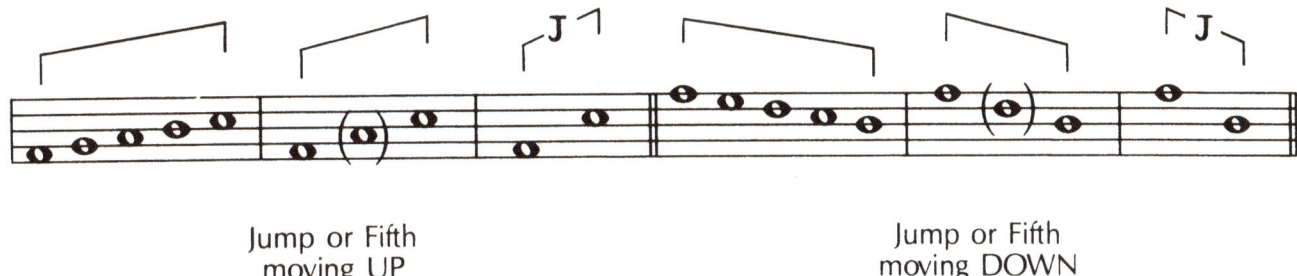

Jump or Fifth
moving UP

Jump or Fifth
moving DOWN

*The Intervals given thus far have been given two types of names: that of the **numerical** distance and a name related to a physical activity. The numerical distance is the traditional system of interval identification, while the **Step and Skip** system is related to the approach taken in my Contemporary Piano and Contemporary Organ Methods.*

*For the beginning student it is often easier to use the **Step** and **Skip** system until the stage where the larger intervals are introduced in Part B of this book. In Part B all intervals are approached from the numerical point of view.*

LESSON SIX

MORE INTERVAL EXERCISES

(1) Name the following intervals as either Skip-Plus-Ones (4ths) or Jumps (5ths). Indicate the direction they are moving with arrows. Use Sk+1 and J, or 4th and 5th.

(2) Name the following intervals as either Sames, Steps, Skips, Skip-Plus-Ones or Jumps. Use arrows to indicate the direction as before.

(3) Circle the Skip-Plus-Ones (Fourths) in this line of notes.

e.g.

(4) Circle the Jumps (Fifths) in this line of notes.

e.g.

(5) Write SKIP-PLUS-ONES moving either UP or DOWN from the given notes depending on the direction of the arrows. Remember the Skip+1's always move from a Line Note to a Space Note or vice-versa.

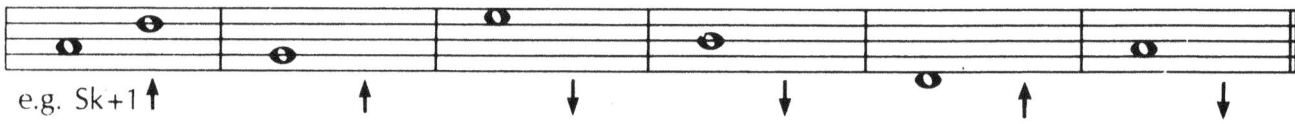

e.g. Sk+1 ↑   ↑   ↓   ↓   ↑   ↓

(6) Write JUMPS moving either UP or DOWN from the given notes depending on the direction of the arrows. Remember that Jumps always move from Line to Line or Space to Space.

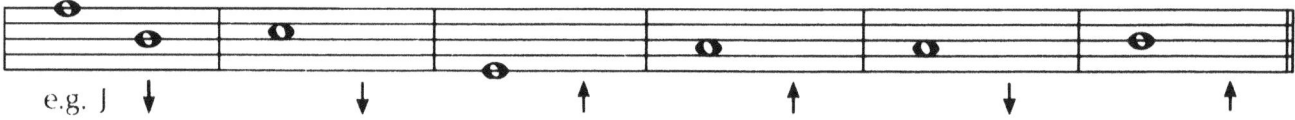

e.g. J ↓   ↓   ↑   ↑   ↓   ↑

LESSON SEVEN

BAR LINES

The upright lines are BAR LINES.

The areas between the bar lines are known as bars or measures.

At the end of a section a **Double Bar** Line is used.

◆◆◆◆◆◆◆◆◆◆◆◆◆◆◆◆◆◆◆◆◆◆◆◆◆◆◆◆◆

EXERCISES

N.B.   Sames = Primes; Steps = Seconds; Skips = Thirds:
Skip-Plus-Ones = Fourths; and Jumps = Fiths.

(1) Write some repeated notes (**same**) next to the given notes.

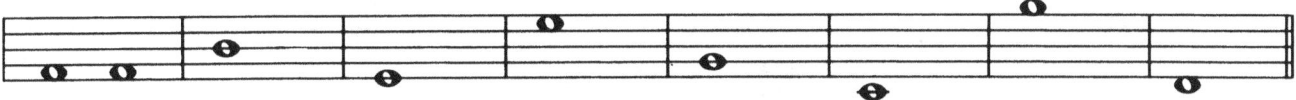

e.g. same

(2) Write some **steps** going **up** from the given notes. Write some **steps** going **down** from the given notes.

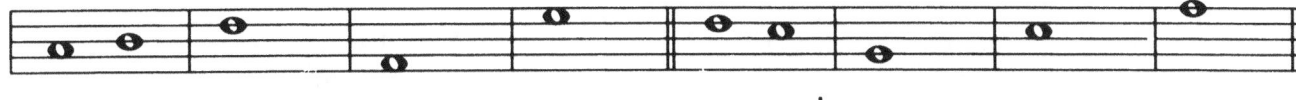

e.g. step ↑   e.g. step ↓

(3) Write **skips up**.   Write **skips down**.

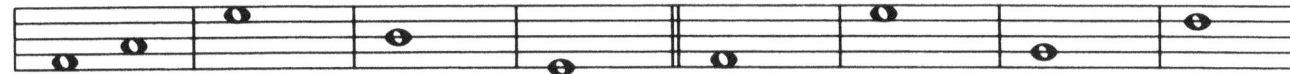

e.g. skip ↑

(4) Write **'skip-plus-1's' up**.   Write **'skip-plus-1's' down**.

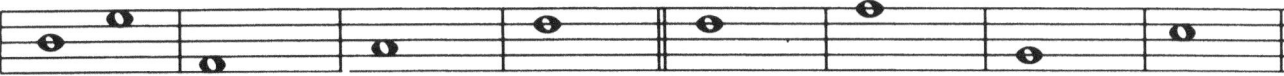

e.g. skip+1 ↑

(5) Write **jumps up**.   Write **jumps down**.

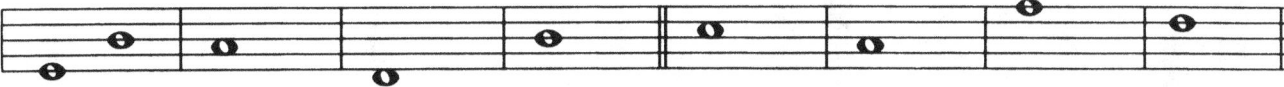

e.g. jump ↑

For more practice in interval writing and naming,
refer to the CTP by Margaret S. Brandman

LESSON EIGHT

NOTE - NAMES

In music we use the first seven letters of the alphabet to identify the sounds. That is: **A B C D E F G.**

The picture of a keyboard below will show how these notes occur and how the sequence is repeated.

LOW SOUNDS　　　　　　　　　　　　　　　　　　　　　　　　　　　**HIGH SOUNDS**

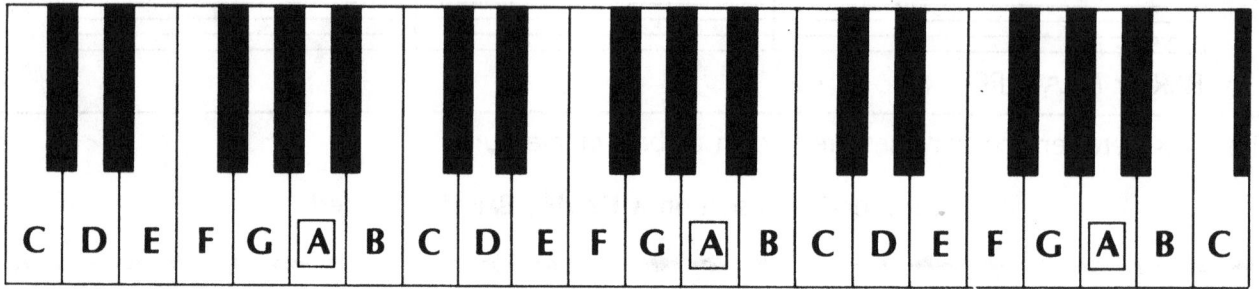

To find your way around a keyboard, memorize the positions of these two notes; **C** and **F**. Then you can move forwards and backwards through the alphabet to find the names of the other notes.

As these two notes are easy to locate on the keyboard, it is useful to think of them as SIGNPOST NOTES.

SIGNPOSTS

'C' is located immediately to the left of the group of TWO black notes.

'F' is located immediately to the LEFT of the group of THREE black notes.

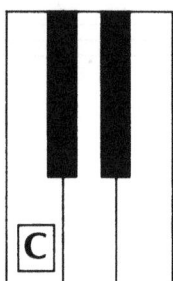
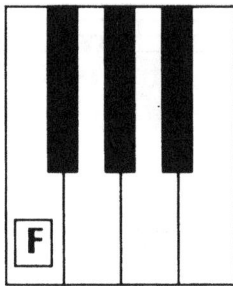

◆◆◆◆◆◆◆◆◆◆◆◆◆◆◆◆◆◆◆◆◆◆◆◆◆◆◆◆◆

EXERCISE

FILL IN THE NAMES FOR THE REST OF THE KEYBOARD.

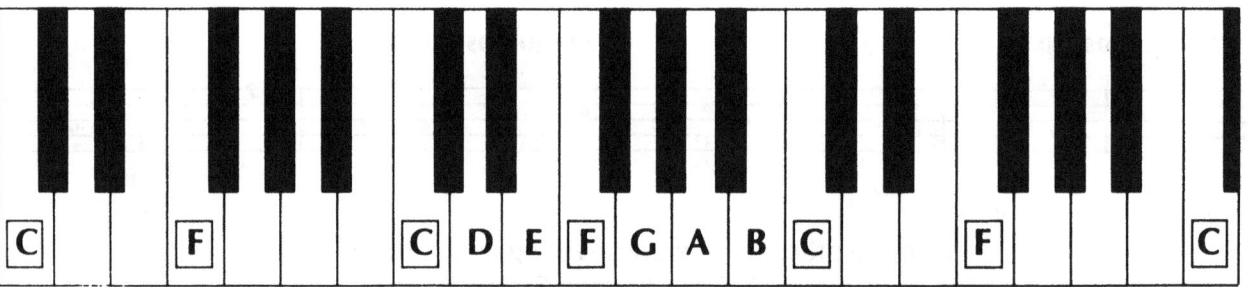

12

LESSON NINE

CLEFS

There are three clefs in use in music today. They are:

 The Treble or G Clef   𝄢 The Bass or F Clef   𝄡 The C Clef. This is a movable clef which is known as either the Soprano, Mezzo-Soprano, Alto, Tenor or Baritone Clef depending upon its position on the Staff.

The C Clef is most frequently used as either the ALTO or TENOR Clef.

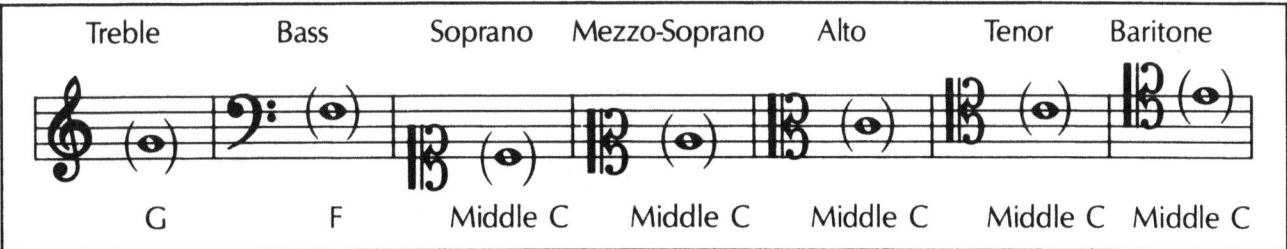

The word CLEF comes from the French word meaning 'key'. The Clef is your 'Front-door key' to the position of the notes on the staff.

SIGNPOST C's

If you learn the position of the note 'C' in relation to each clef, you will be able to find your position on your instrument and then be able to continue reading by intervals from the Signpost note.

Here is a picture of a keyboard and the location and pitch (sound) of the Signpost C's in the various Clefs.

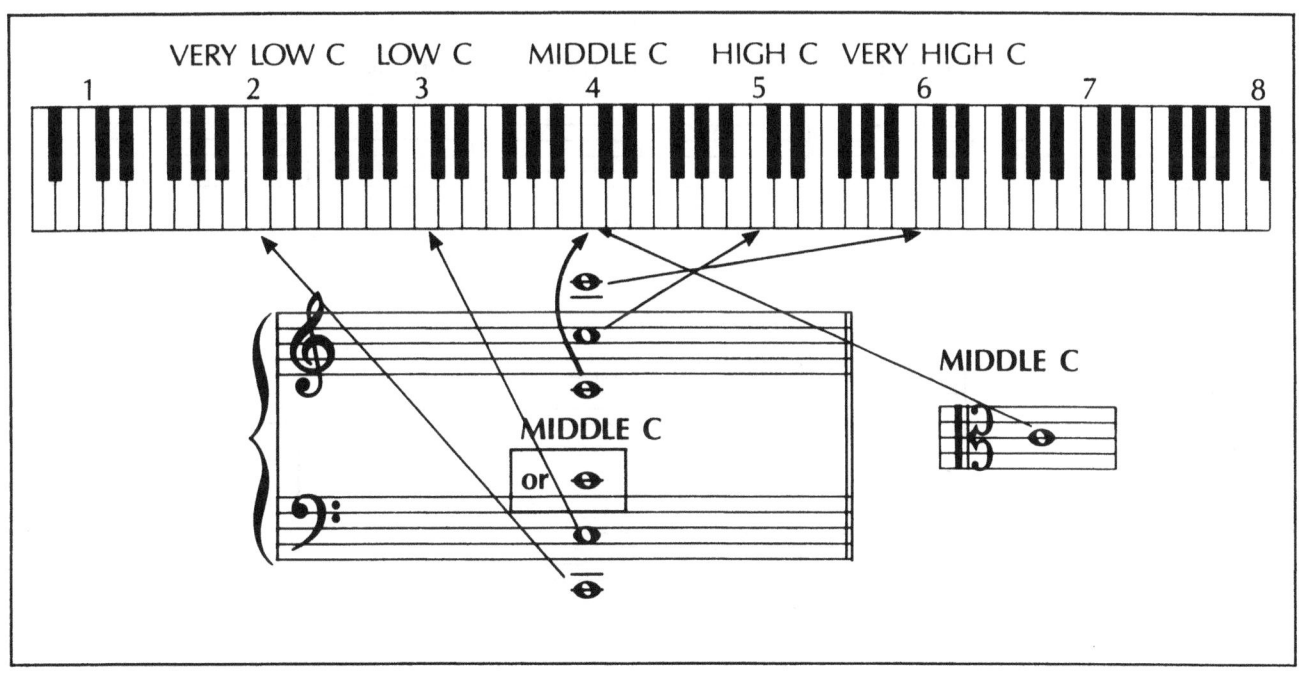

◆◆◆◆◆◆◆◆◆◆◆◆◆◆◆◆

EXERCISE

Name the following Clefs.

1. 𝄢 ....   2. 𝄡 ....   3. 𝄞 ....

LESSON TEN

WRITING PRACTICE
CLEFS AND BRACES

Draw Treble Clefs

Draw Bass Clefs

Draw C Clefs as Alto Clefs (Printed Style)

Draw C Clefs as Tenor Clefs (Alternate style, easier for handwritten music).

Draw Braces {

Draw Braces and Clefs.

LESSON ELEVEN

THE TREBLE CLEF

The Treble Clef sign (𝄞) is in fact a stylised or fancy letter G. It shows that the note G above the middle C is placed on the second line of the Staff and that all the other notes take their placement from this given note. It is used for Voices and instruments which mainly use notes from Middle C and higher. For instance the Soprano voice and instruments such as the Violin, Trumpet and Guitar.

(a) Here is the staff with the Treble Clef placed upon it and the location of Middle C and High C in relation to the Clef.

(b) An easy way to remember the location of the two Sign post C's, is to imagine a line drawn through the ball of the Clef for Middle C, and imagine High C sitting on the top of the Treble Clef's curl.

The names of the notes in the exercises below can be gauged by intervals from either of the two C's. Here are the alphabetical names as they occur on the keyboard for you to use as a means of figuring out the note names. Remember that when used in alphabetical order they indicate notes which rise in pitch, and when used in reverse order they indicate notes which fall in pitch.

$$A \quad B \quad C \quad D \quad E \quad F \quad G \quad A \quad B \quad C \quad D \quad E \quad F \quad G$$

A STEP moves to the next letter name along the line, while a SKIP leaves out one letter.
For Example:

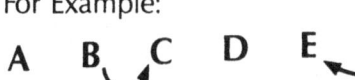  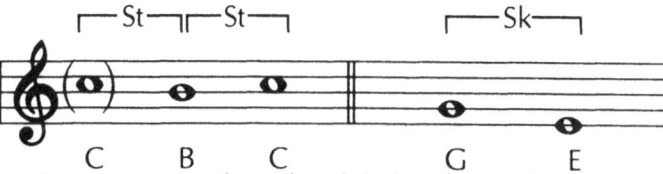

Figure out the intervals in the questions below by using your pencil on the alphabet list to draw Step and Skip arrows.

◆◆◆◆◆◆◆◆◆◆◆◆◆◆◆◆◆◆◆◆◆◆◆◆◆◆◆◆◆

EXERCISES

(1) Write the names of these Treble Clef notes, using the Signpost C's as a means of locating your position on the Staff, then moving by INTERVALS of a Step or Skip from note to note to work out the other names. Write the intervals between the brackets above the notes and the alphabetical note-names in the spaces provided below the notes.

....

(2) Write these notes, by first working out the intervals between their alphabetical names. The arrows show the direction in which the notes should move.

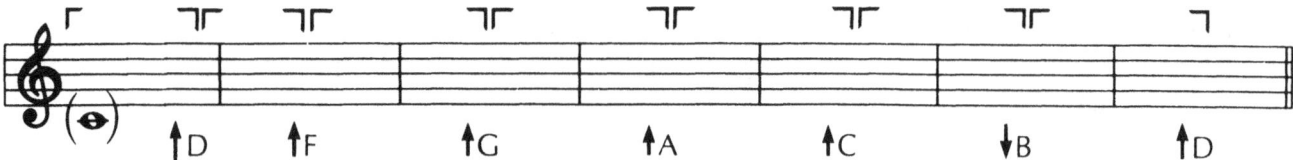

LESSON TWELVE

THE BASS CLEF

The Bass Clef sign (𝄢) is a stylised or fancy letter F. It shows the placement of the note F below middle C, on the fourth line of the Staff. It is used for instruments and voices which mainly use notes from middle C down. For instance the Baritone voice and the Bass voice and the 'Cello, Double Bass, Electric Bass and Bassoon.

(a) Here is the staff with the Bass Clef placed upon it and the location of Middle C and Low C in relation to the Clef.

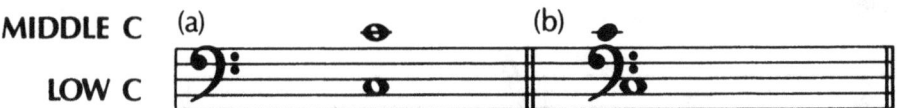

(b) An easy way to remember the location of the two Sign post C's, is to imagine Middle C as a Bowler Hat sitting above the Staff, and to view Low C sitting under the dots.

To gauge the names of notes which are a FOURTH or SKIP-PLUS-ONE from each other, move along the letter names in this fashion:

To gauge the names of notes which are a FIFTH or JUMP apart, move along the letter names in the following fashion:

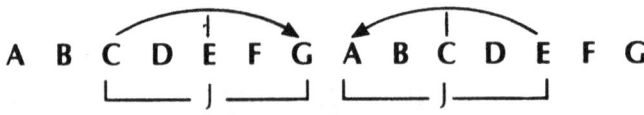 

◆◆◆◆◆◆◆◆◆◆◆◆◆◆◆◆◆◆◆◆◆◆◆◆◆◆◆◆◆

EXERCISES

(1) a) Indicate the interval between each note between the brackets above the staff.
    b) Work out the note-names using the intervals and the alphabetical list above.

(2) a) Work out the interval between each given letter name.
    b) Write the notes following the interval sizes.

(3) Work out the intervals and write the notes as before.

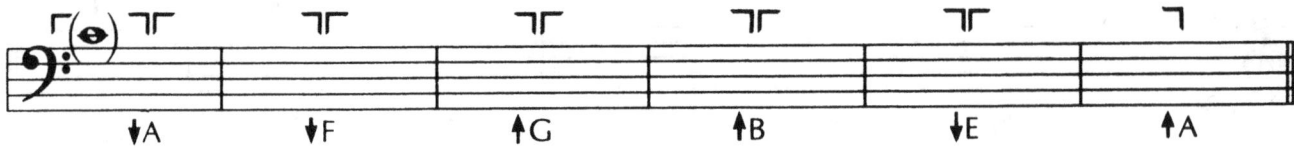

LESSON THIRTEEN

THE ALTO AND TENOR CLEFS

The sign for both the Alto and Tenor Clef is the C Clef (𝄡) which itself is a stylised or fancy letter C.
A version of the clef which is easier to write by hand, looks like this. 𝄡
When the C Clef is placed on the **middle** line of the staff it is known as the **Alto Clef**.
When the C Clef is placed on the **fourth** line of the staff it is known as the **Tenor Clef**.
The Alto Clef is primarily used for the Viola whose range of notes is centred around Middle C and enables the composer or arranger to avoid the use of multiple leger lines.
The Tenor Clef is found in music for Bassoon, Tenor Trombone, 'Cello and Double Bass.

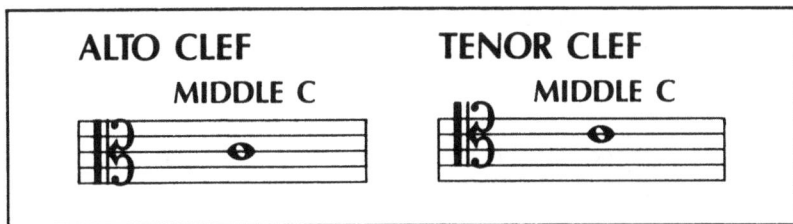

It is handy to know how to read music in C clef if you ever wish to read or play orchestral score parts on your instrument. Skills in reading in C Clef can be an aid to transposition.

Do not try to memorise the note-names in each clef, simply read by intervals and use the same reading system in each clef.

Here is an alphabetical list to help you work out the names in the following questions.

A B C D E F G A B C D E F G

◆-◆-◆-◆-◆-◆-◆-◆-◆-◆-◆-◆-◆-◆-◆-◆-◆-◆-◆

EXERCISES

(1) a) Write the intervals between the brackets above the notes.
   b) Using Middle C on the THIRD line as your Signpost note, work out the note-names.

ALTO CLEF

(2) a) Write the intervals above.
   b) Work out the note names, using Middle C on the FOURTH line as your Signpost note.

TENOR CLEF

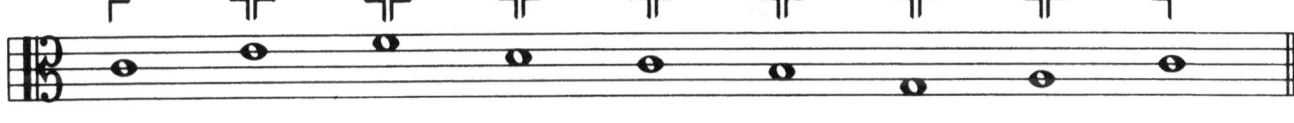

(3) Write these notes by first working out the intervals between their alphabetical names. The arrows show the direction in which the notes should move.

LESSON FOURTEEN

THE GREAT STAFF

The Great Staff is an eleven line staff made up of a Treble Staff and a Bass Staff plus the extra leger line for Middle C, all joined by a brace. It is also known as the Grand Staff.

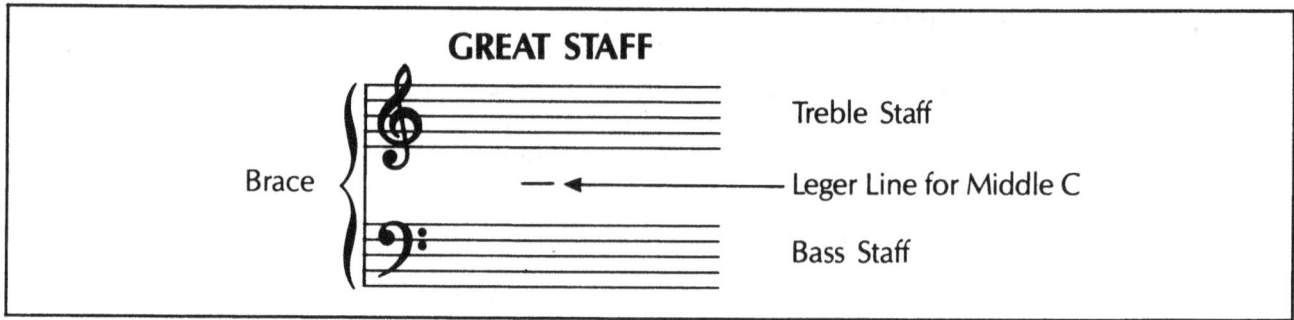

Notes covering the entire vocal range can be shown on the Great Staff, and as it covers such a wide range it is used by such instruments as the Piano, Organ, Harp and Piano Accordion which can play both Low and High range Notes.

Middle C can be seen to be centrally located between the two Staves, which is why it is called Middle C!

The note G around which the Treble Clef curls, is exactly a Fifth or Jump higher than Middle C, while the note F that the Bass Clef denotes, is exactly a Fifth lower than Middle C.

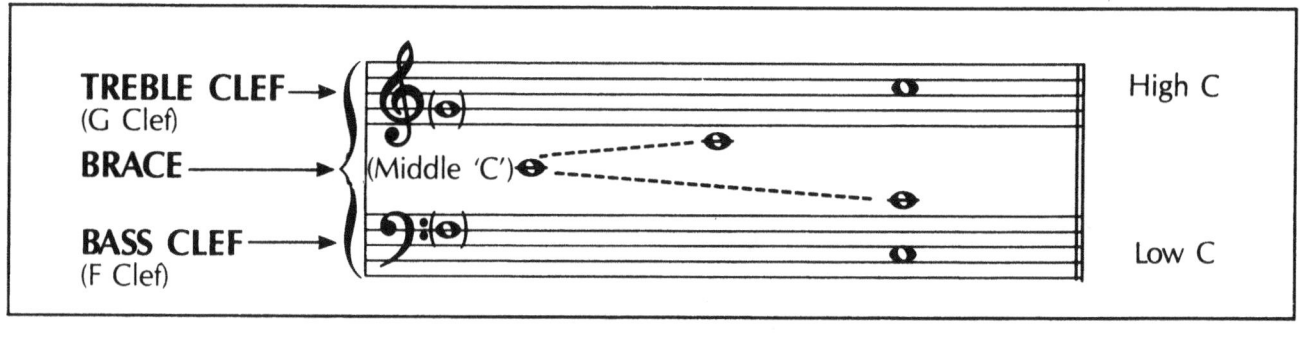

EXERCISES

Name these notes on the Great Staff. Work by intervals from the Signpost C's.

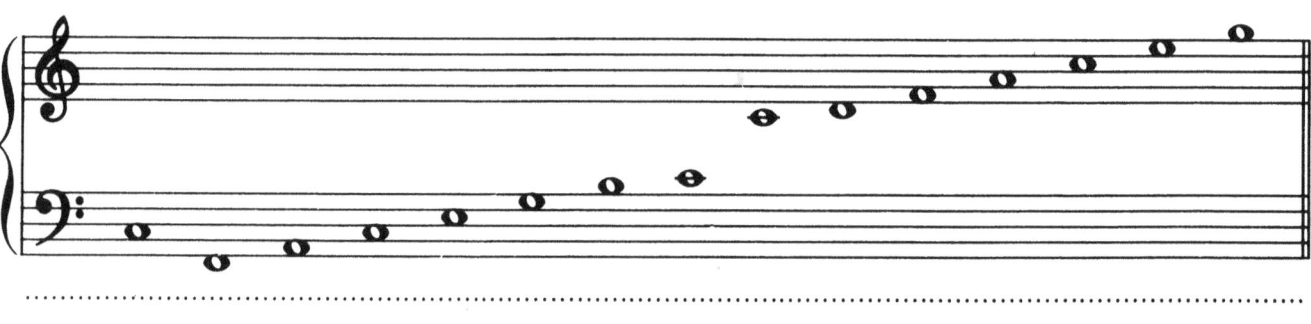

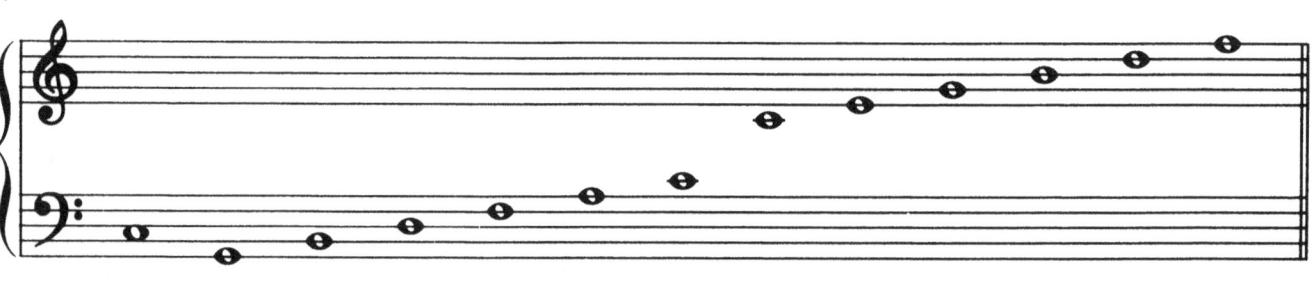

LESSON FIFTEEN

MORE NOTE-NAMING AND WRITING ON THE GREAT STAFF AND IN C CLEF

(1) Name the notes on this Great Staff.
Work by intervals from the Signpost C's and then from each note to the next.

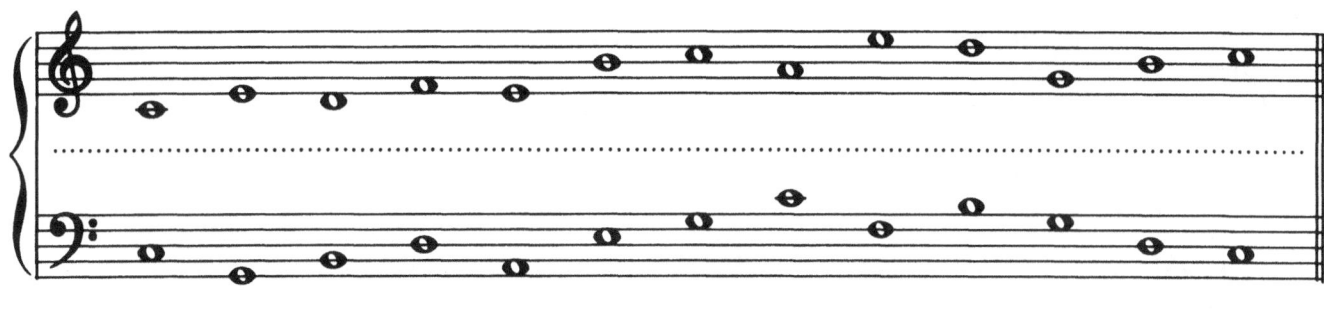

(2) a) Indicate the intervals between the notes above the staff.
b) Write the required notes on this Alto Staff.

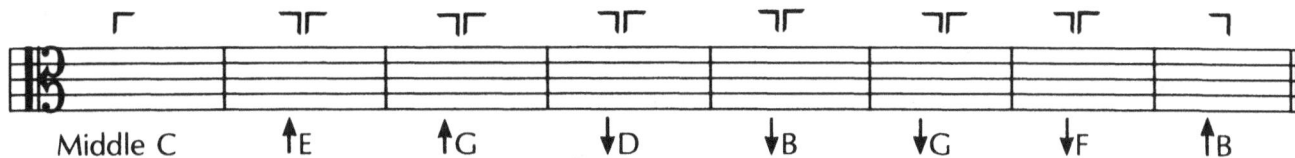

(3) Write two each of the required notes on the Great Staff, one on the Bass Staff and one on the Treble Staff.

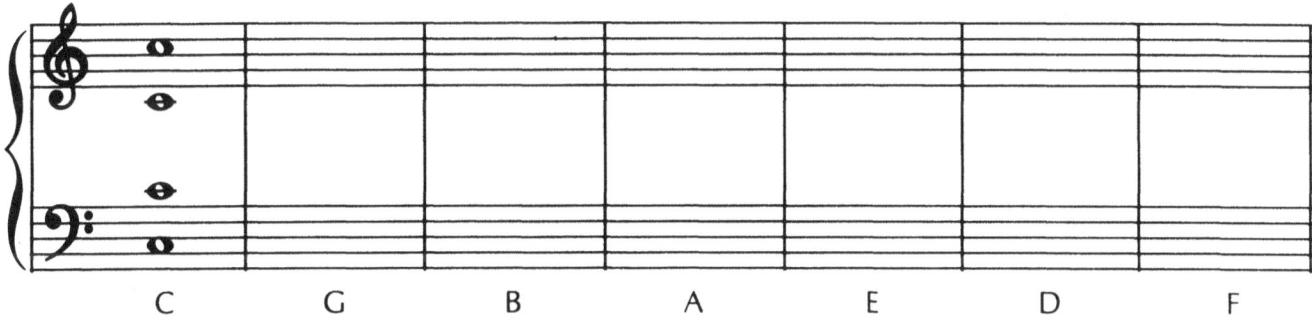

(4) a) Indicate the intervals between the notes above the staff.
b) Write the required notes on this Tenor Staff.

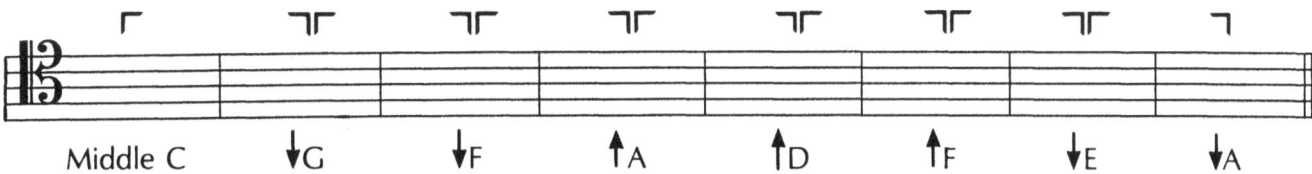

(5) Work out the note names of these notes on the Alto and Tenor Staves, using the interval system as before.

LESSON SIXTEEN

NOTES AND RESTS

In music we use several different shaped NOTES to indicate the length of time or duration of a musical **sound**.

Each note value has a matching REST which indicates the same duration or length of time of silence.

Below are four of these notes and rests and their common time-values. There are two ways they can be named:
1. The North American system which labels each note as a fraction of the largest note value and,
2. The British system which uses names handed down from the Medieval names for notes.
The following list gives both names.

NOTE-SHAPE	AMERICAN NAME	BRITISH NAME	DURATION	REST-SHAPE
o	Whole Note	Semibreve	4 counts	▬ (on line)
𝅗𝅥	Half Note	Minim	2 counts	▬ (on line)
♩	Quarter Note	Crotchet	1 count	𝄽
♪	Eighth Note	Quaver	½ of 1 count	𝄾

SPECIAL NOTE
It is convention to use the Whole Rest/Semibreve Rest. ▬ Whenever an entire bar's rest is needed in **any** Time-Signature.

◆◆◆◆◆◆◆◆◆◆◆◆◆◆◆◆◆◆◆◆◆◆◆◆◆◆◆◆◆◆

EXERCISE

Identify the following notes and rests.

e.g. 𝅗𝅥 = Half Note or Minim,   𝄽 = Quarter Rest or Crotchet Rest.

1. o   = ...
2. ▬ (whole rest) = ...
3. ♩   = ...
4. 𝄾   = ...

5. 𝅗𝅥   = ...
6. ♪   = ...
7. ▬ (half rest) = ...
8. 𝄽   = ...

LESSON SEVENTEEN

WRITING PRACTICE
NOTES AND RESTS

Draw Whole Notes (Semibreves)

Draw Whole Rests (Semibreve Rests)

Draw Half Notes (Minims)

Draw Half Rests (Minim Rests)

Draw Quarter Notes (Crotchets)

Draw Quarter Rests (Crotchet Rests)

Draw Eighth Notes (Quavers)

Draw Eighth Rests (Quaver Rests)

Two or more quavers can be joined together by a beam.

Draw Beamed Quavers

LESSON EIGHTEEN

TIME-VALUES

The number of counts each note receives can be shown by boxes drawn under the notes which can be shaded in or coloured in to represent the duration of the sound.

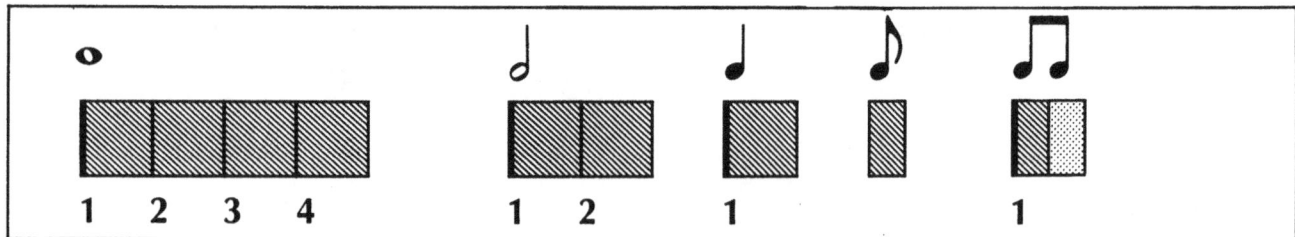

Rests can be represented by similar boxes left unshaded or blank.

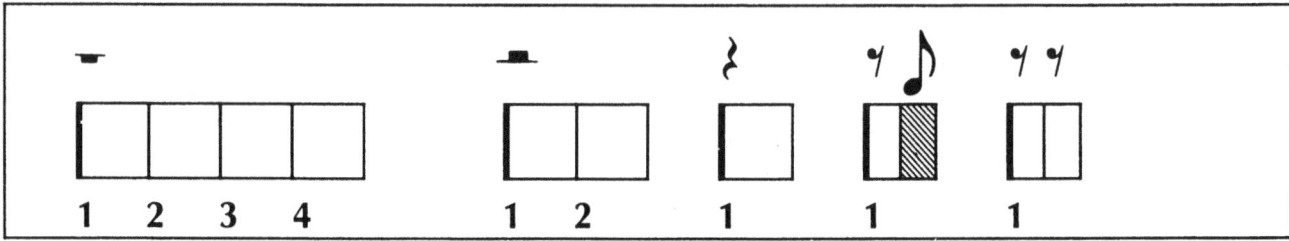

A colour system to use is given in both my Contemporary Piano and Contemporary Organ Methods, plus in the CTP.

When eight quavers are used in a bar where the quarter note or crotchet is the beat note, they can be counted by using the word 'AND' (& or +) on the second quaver of each pair.

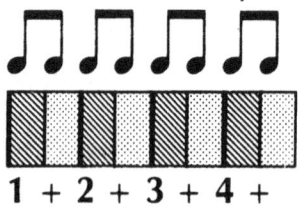

◆◆◆◆◆◆◆◆◆◆◆◆◆◆◆◆◆◆◆◆◆◆◆◆◆◆◆◆◆◆◆◆◆◆

EXERCISES

(1) How many counts do each of the following receive?

1. 𝄺 = ...   6. 𝄻 = ...

2. 𝄽 = ...   7. ♪ = ...

3. ♩ + ♩ = ...   8. ♩ = ...

4. 𝅗𝅥 = ...   9. 𝄾 = ...

5. 𝅝 = ...   10. ♫ = ...

(2) Draw the following notes and rests:

1. A one-count note ....   5. A two-count note ....

2. A two-count rest ....   6. A one-count rest ....

3. A half-count note ....   7. A four-count note ....

4. A four-count rest ....   8. A half-count rest ....

22

LESSON NINETEEN

DOTTED NOTES AND DOTTED RESTS

A dot after a note extends the note by half of the original value of the note.

The Semibreve or Whole Note (𝑜) = 4 counts. The Dotted Semibreve (𝑜·) = (4+2) = 6 counts.

𝑜

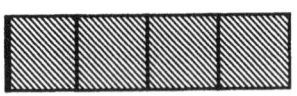

1   2   3   4

𝑜·

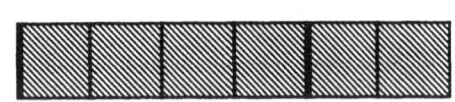

1 + 2 + 3 + 4 + 1 + 2 +

The Minim or Half Note (𝅗𝅥) = 2 counts. The Dotted Minim (𝅗𝅥·) = (2+1) = 3 counts.

𝅗𝅥

1   2

𝅗𝅥·

1 + 2 + 3 +

The Crotchet or Quarter Note (♩) = 1 count. The Dotted Crotchet (♩·) = (1+½) = 1½ counts.

♩

1

♩·

1 + 2

Rests may also be dotted.

A Dotted Semibreve Rest would receive 6 counts.   ▬· = 6

A Dotted Minim Rest would receive 3 counts.   ▬· = 3

A Dotted Crotchet Rest would receive 1½ counts.   𝄽· = 1½

◆◆◆◆◆◆◆◆◆◆◆◆◆◆◆◆◆◆◆◆◆◆◆◆◆◆◆

EXERCISE

How many counts do these notes and rests receive?

1. 𝑜· = ...
2. 𝅗𝅥 + 𝅗𝅥 = ...
3. 𝅗𝅥· = ...
4. ▬ = ...
5. 𝄽· = ...

6. ♩· = ...
7. ▬· = ...
8. 𝅗𝅥· + 𝅗𝅥 = ...
9. ▬· = ...
10. ♩· + ♪ = ...

LESSON TWENTY

TIME-SIGNATURE

Notes of different time-values can be grouped together in various arrangements.

Bar lines are used to show the divisions between groups of notes.

The grouping of counts into bars is indicated by the Time-Signature (simply a long word for Time-Sign) which appears at the beginning of a piece of music.

The TOP Number in the Time-Signature tells HOW MANY counts in each bar.

For Example: 2, 3, 4, 6 etc.

The LOWER Number tells WHAT KIND of note receives one count.

For Example: a half note $\frac{1}{2}$ ♩   a quarter note $\frac{1}{4}$ ♩   an eighth note $\frac{1}{8}$ ♪

The lower number represents the lower half of the fraction.

For Example: $\frac{2}{4}$ = 2 × a $\frac{1}{4}$ note (♩)
(times)

and $\frac{6}{8}$ = 6 × an $\frac{1}{8}$ note (♪)

and $\frac{4}{2}$ = 4 × a $\frac{1}{2}$ note (𝅗𝅥)

◆◆◆◆◆◆◆◆◆◆◆◆◆◆◆◆◆◆◆◆◆◆◆◆◆

EXERCISE

Place the number of notes in the first box and complete the fraction for the type of note in the second blank box, then copy both numbers in order to write the time-signatures.

1. ♩ ♩ ♩ [3] × $\frac{1}{4}$ = $\frac{3}{4}$

2. 𝅗𝅥 𝅗𝅥 ☐ × $\frac{1}{☐}$ = $\frac{☐}{☐}$

3. ♪♪♪♪ ☐ × $\frac{1}{☐}$ = $\frac{☐}{☐}$

4. 𝅗𝅥 𝅗𝅥 𝅗𝅥 𝅗𝅥 ☐ × $\frac{1}{☐}$ = $\frac{☐}{☐}$

5. ♪♪♪ ☐ × $\frac{1}{☐}$ = $\frac{☐}{☐}$

6. ♩ ♩ ☐ × $\frac{1}{☐}$ = $\frac{☐}{☐}$

7. ♪ ♪ ☐ × $\frac{1}{☐}$ = $\frac{☐}{☐}$

8. ♩♩♩♩ ☐ × $\frac{1}{☐}$ = $\frac{☐}{☐}$

9. 𝅗𝅥 𝅗𝅥 𝅗𝅥 ☐ × $\frac{1}{☐}$ = $\frac{☐}{☐}$

Colour highlight the lower number of each time signature, using the standard colours given in the introduction.

LESSON TWENTY-ONE

SIMPLE TIME

Time-Signatures which can be described as SIMPLE TIME all have **undotted** notes as **Beat Notes**. That is, Beat Notes which divide into two equal parts, such as minims (𝅗𝅥), crotchets (♩) or quavers (♪). Each of the subdivisions is called a **Pulse**, therefore in Simple Time there are **two** Pulses per Beat Note.

For Example: in 4/4 time there are four **Beat Notes** which divide into eight **Pulses**.

When TWO undotted beat notes are grouped together in each bar, the Time-Signature is called SIMPLE DUPLE time. (Duple means two)

EXAMPLE 2/4 ♩ ♩ | ♩ ♩ ||
         1 2   1 2

When THREE undotted beat notes are grouped together in each bar, the Time-Signature is called SIMPLE TRIPLE time. (Triple means three)

EXAMPLE 3/4 ♩ ♩ ♩ | ♩ ♩ ♩ ||
         1 2 3   1 2 3

When FOUR undotted beat notes are grouped together in each bar, the Time-Signature is called SIMPLE QUADRUPLE time. (Quadruple means four)

EXAMPLE 4/4 ♩ ♩ ♩ ♩ | ♩ ♩ ♩ ♩ ||
         1 2 3 4   1 2 3 4

The three time-signatures given here are some of the most frequently used time-signatures.

2/4 Can be used for Marches and has an accent or emphasis on the first of each two beats. The sign for a strong accent is >

EXAMPLE 2/4 ♩> ♩ | ♩> ♩ ||

3/4 Can be used for Waltzes and has an accent on the first of each group of three.

EXAMPLE 3/4 ♩> ♩ ♩ | ♩> ♩ ♩ ||

4/4 Can be used for dance music and other music in a wide variety of styles. In this time-signature a strong accent occurs on the first beat of each bar and a medium accent on the third beat of each bar. The sign for a medium accent is —

EXAMPLE 4/4 ♩> ♩ ♩— ♩ | ♩> ♩ ♩— ♩ ||

C = Common Time. This sign is often used as a substitute for 4/4 time.

LESSON TWENTY-TWO

MORE ON TIMING

- Write the **counts** under the notes
- Space the counts out evenly throughout the bar
- Use numbers only when these note values are given: o, d., d, ♩
- Use numbers and 'ands' (+) for the entire segment when any quavers occur

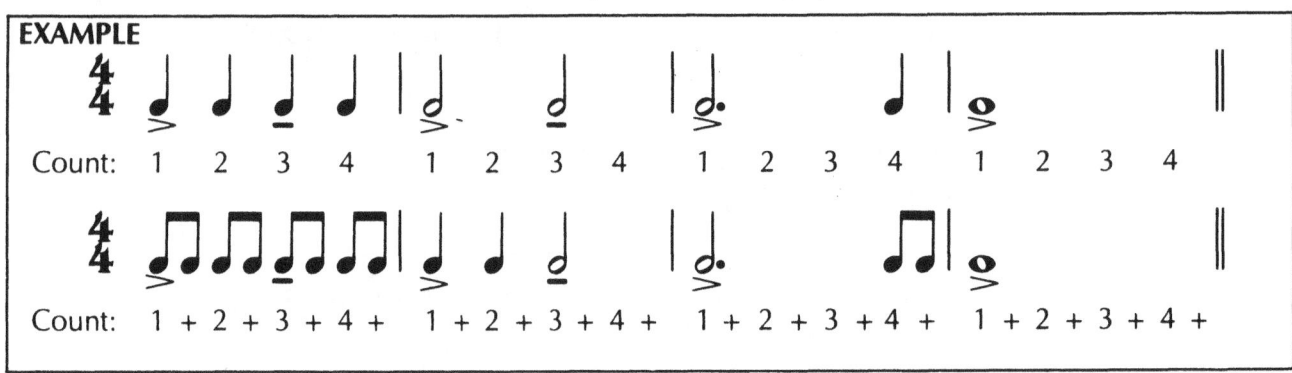

EXERCISES

(1) Write the counts under the notes.

(2) Write the counts under the notes and divide the notes into the bars.

LESSON TWENTY-THREE

GROUPING OF NOTES AND RESTS

In 4/4 time it is wise to group all notes and rests so that the bar can be seen to fall into two halves. Think of the bar as having an imaginary line in the middle.

Do not cross the middle of the bar when beaming quavers or combining note values.

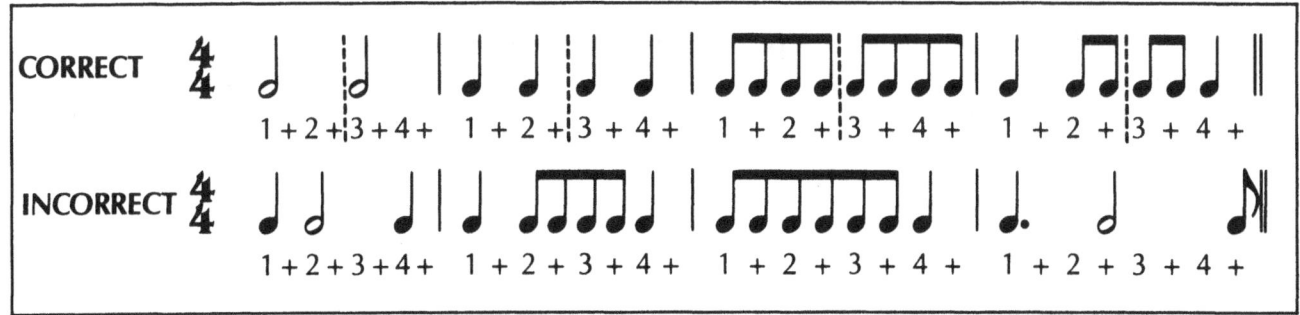

When using RESTS in 3/4 time, use the combined minim rest for beats 1 and 2 and use only separate crotchet rests for beats 2 and 3 so that the eye can clearly see the three beats. **

*Use Semibreve Rest for a whole-bar's rest in any Time-signature.

Refer to Lesson 16.

EXERCISES

(1) Supply the time-signatures and write the counts for these examples.

(2) Supply the time-signatures, add the bar lines and write the counts for these examples.

** Special Note: Some examination bodies stipulate that for the first two beats in ¾ time, only quarter rests (crotchet rests) should be used.

LESSON TWENTY-FOUR

FILL IN THE MISSING NOTES AND RESTS

SECTION ONE - NOTES

First write the counts evenly spaced throughout the bars following the style given in the first bar in each line. Then add NOTES of the correct value to complete the bars.

Group the notes according to the counts and take care not to cross the middle of the bar in $\frac{4}{4}$ time.

Use the same principle when grouping notes in $\frac{2}{4}$ as well.

EXAMPLE — This bar has only one crotchet worth one count. As it is $\frac{3}{4}$ time the bar should have three counts. Add a note or notes worth two counts to complete the bar. i.e. 1× 𝅗𝅥, or 2× ♩ or 4× ♪ or other combinations of ♪'s and 𝅗𝅥's.

SECTION TWO — RESTS

First write the counts evenly spaced throughout the bars. Then add RESTS of the correct value to complete the bars.

Complete each count in turn and remember the grouping rules for Rests in $\frac{3}{4}$ time. (See Lesson 23)

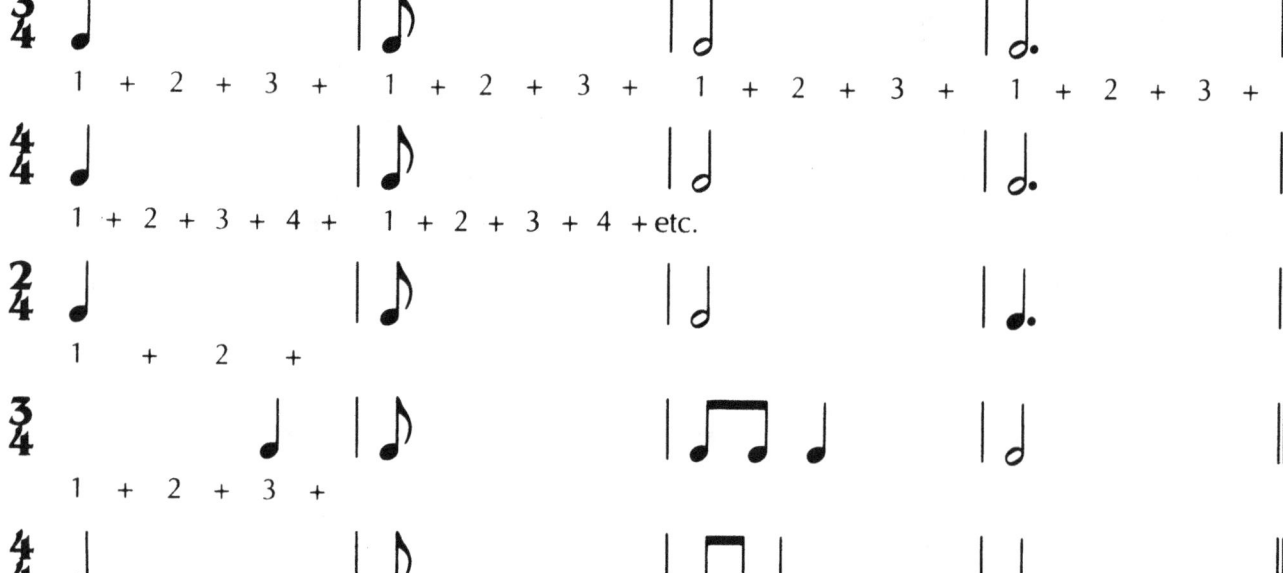

LESSON TWENTY-FIVE

STEMS AND BEAMS

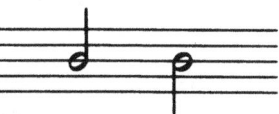

If a note is written on the MIDDLE line, its stem can go either up or down.

If the note-head is written lower than the Middle line, then the stem must go UP on the Right Hand side of the note-head

FOR EXAMPLE:

If the note-head is written higher than the Middle line, then the stem must go DOWN on the Left Hand side of the note-head.

FOR EXAMPLE: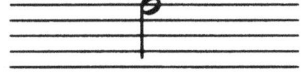

If a group of quavers need to be beamed together, decide on the direction of the majority of note stems and use this as a guide to beaming the notes. Remember to beam quavers together according to the counts and not to cross the middle of the bar in $\frac{4}{4}$ time.

e.g.

◆◆◆◆◆◆◆◆◆◆◆◆◆◆◆◆◆◆◆◆◆◆◆◆◆◆◆◆◆◆

EXERCISE

Add stems and beams to the following notes.

1 + 2 + 3 + 4 +   1 + 2 + 3 + 4 +   1 + 2 + 3 + 4 +   1 + 2 + 3 + 4 +

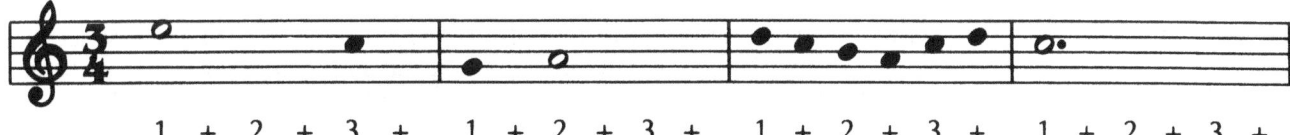

1 + 2 + 3 +   1 + 2 + 3 +   1 + 2 + 3 +   1 + 2 + 3 +

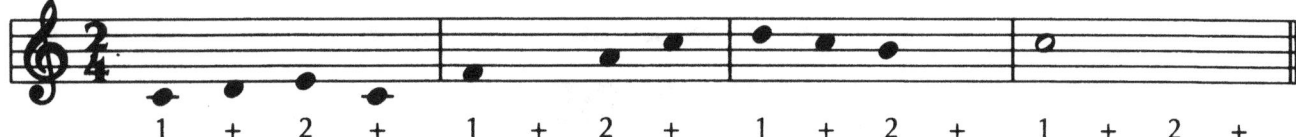

1 + 2 +   1 + 2 +   1 + 2 +   1 + 2 +

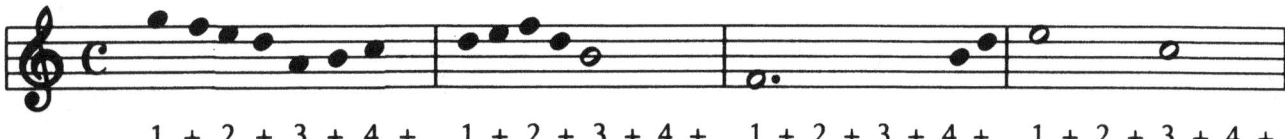

1 + 2 + 3 + 4 +   1 + 2 + 3 + 4 +   1 + 2 + 3 + 4 +   1 + 2 + 3 + 4 +

LESSON TWENTY-SIX

WHOLE TONES AND SEMITONES

Apart from what we already know as steps between the notes, there are also two different types of steps: Half Steps or Semitones (S) and Whole Steps or Tones (W)

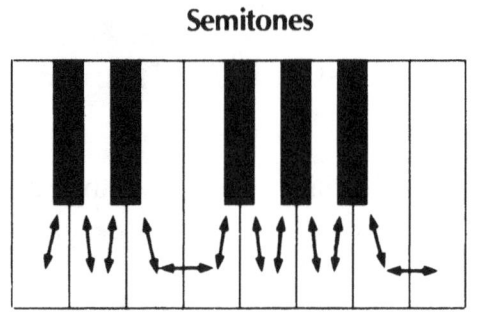

The Semitone is the smallest distance between any two notes on the keyboard. It is the distance from one note to the very next nearest be it black or white.

The entire keyboard consists of semitones between each note.

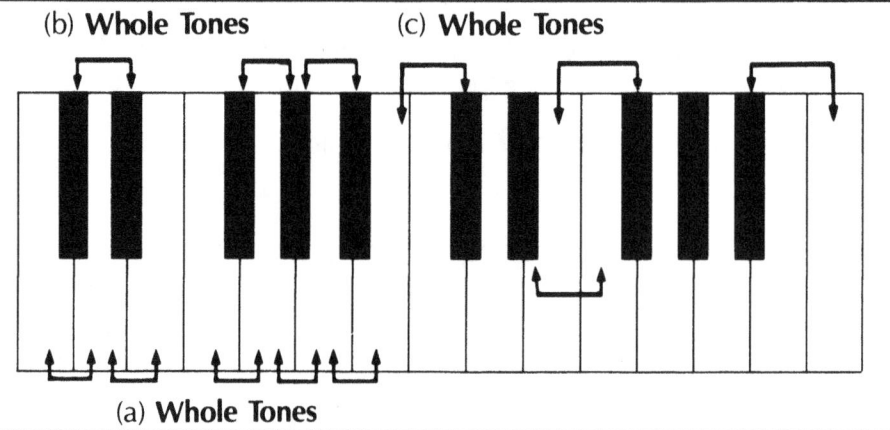

Whole Tones are twice the distance of Semitones. Miss out one key only. There are Whole Tones between most white keys (a) and between the black keys in the two groups (b). Where there are two white keys together, Whole tones travel from black key to white key or vice-versa (c).

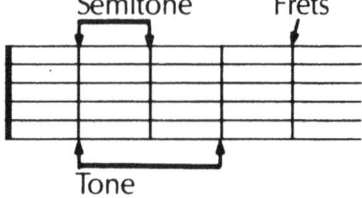

On a fretted instrument a semitone is the distance from one fret to the next, and a whole tone is twice as far.

SHARP (♯), FLAT (♭) AND NATURAL (♮).

The sign used when a note has to be raised a semitone is a Sharp (♯). If the note is to be lowered a semitone a Flat is used (♭). If either of these has to be cancelled, a Natural sign is used (♮). The Natural brings the note back to the ordinary white note on the keyboard. Collectively these signs are called **Accidentals**.

An Accidental must be written on exactly the same line or space as the note to which it refers.

◆◆◆◆◆◆◆◆◆◆◆◆◆◆◆◆◆◆◆◆◆◆◆◆◆◆◆◆◆◆◆

EXERCISE

Write Sharps, Flats and Natural Signs in front of the given notes.

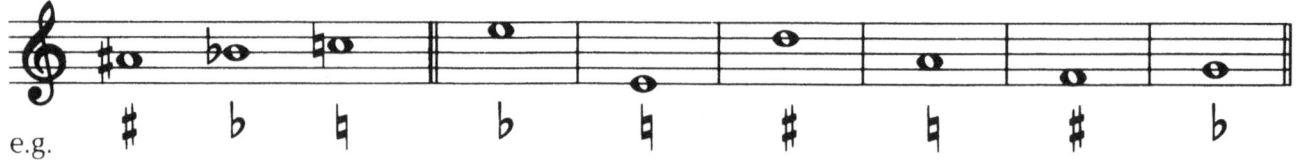

LESSON TWENTY-SEVEN

SHARPS

> ♯ A Sharp is a sign which indicates that a note has to be raised by a semitone.

As we saw in Lesson 26.

A semitone is the distance from one note to the very next nearest, the entire keyboard consists of semitones between each note.

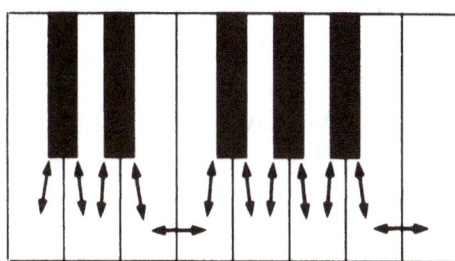

A SHARPENED note is played on the very next key to the right.

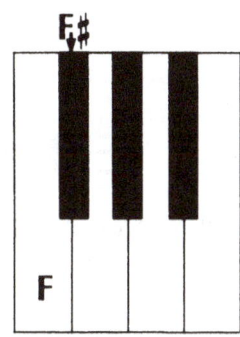
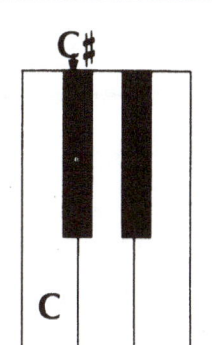

Accidentals are written immediately to the left (in front of) the note on the staff. However when we refer to the note by its letter name when speaking or writing the alphabetical name of the note, we place the accidental after the letter name (immediately to the right). For example F♯ (F sharp) or B♭ (B Flat) **not** Sharp F or Flat B.

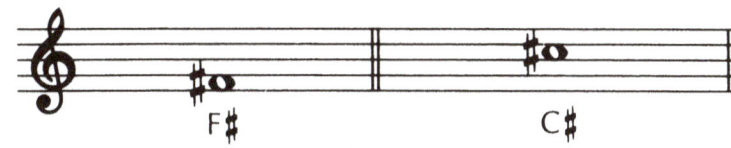

◆◆◆◆◆◆◆◆◆◆◆◆◆◆◆◆◆◆◆◆◆◆◆◆◆◆◆◆◆◆

EXERCISE

First write the intervals between the notes in the bracketted area above the notes.

Then write in the name of the Sharpened note in the space provided and darken the correct key in the pictures above.

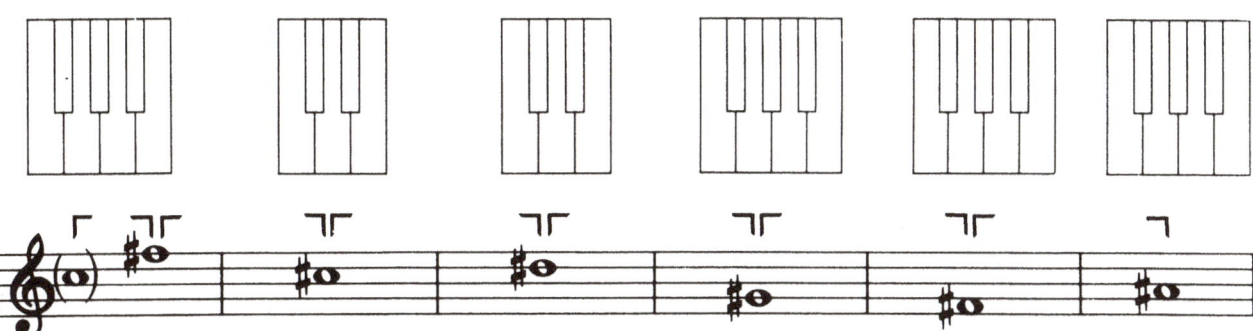

31

LESSON TWENTY-EIGHT

FLATS

♭ A flat is a sign which indicates that a note has to be lowered by a semitone.

A FLATTENED note is played on the very next key to the left.

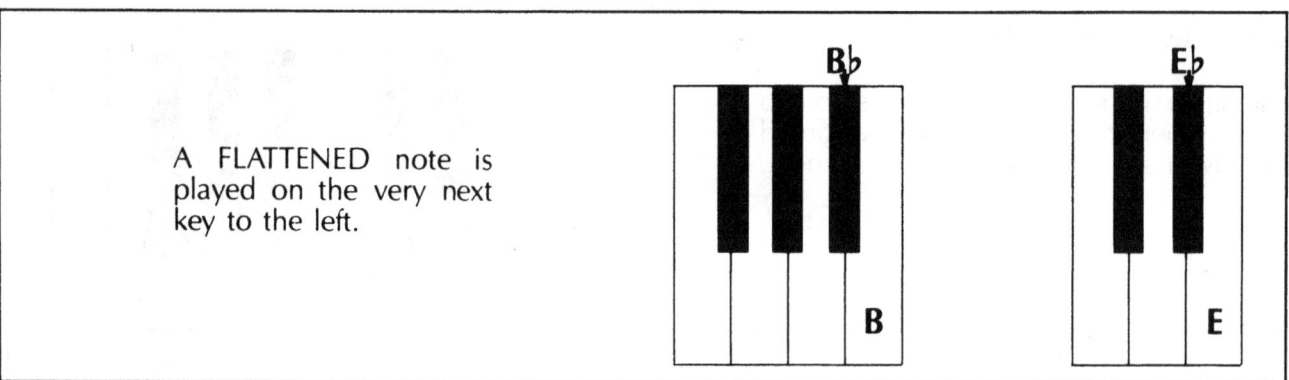

EXERCISES

First write the intervals between the notes in the bracketted areas above the staff.

Then write in the name of the Flattened or Sharpened note in the space provided below the staff and darken the correct key in the pictures above.

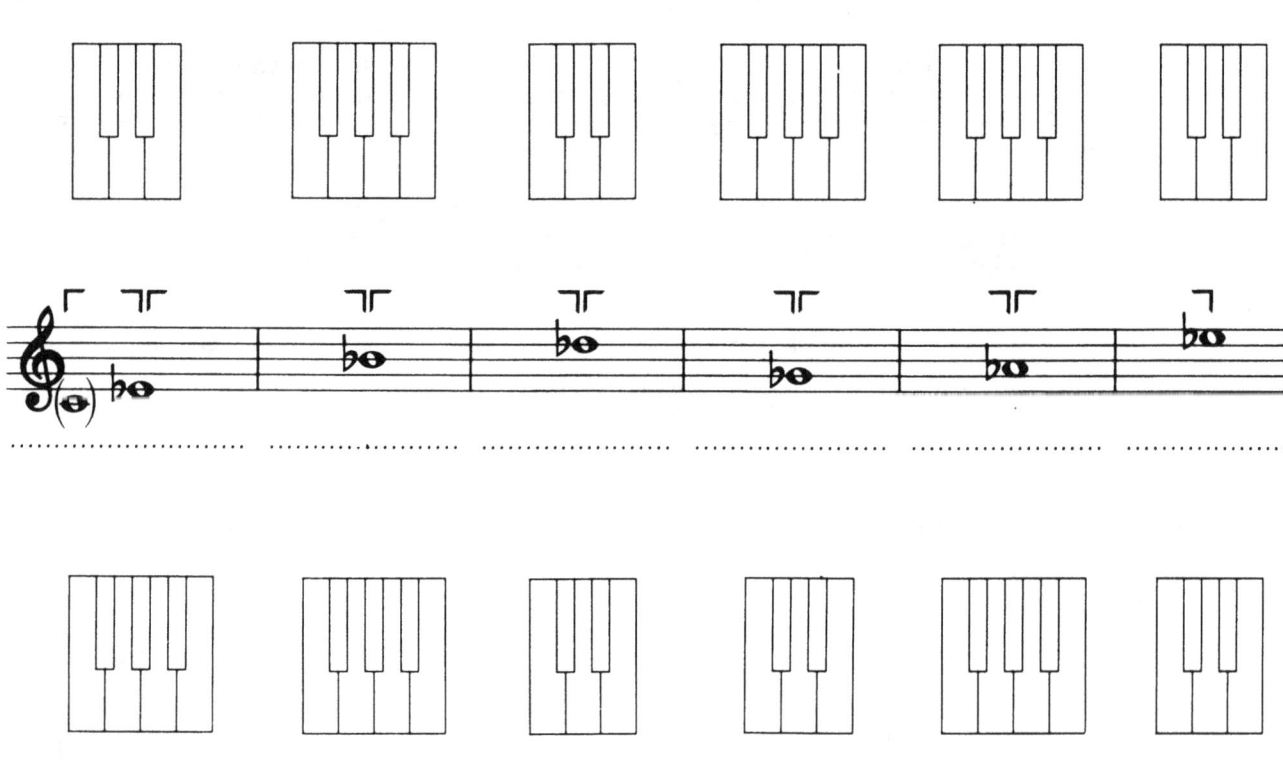

LESSON TWENTY-NINE

MORE ON SHARPS AND FLATS

As we saw earlier, a Sharpened note moves to the very next key to the right and a Flattened note moves to the very next key to the left.
Accordingly, the pairs of white notes which are not separated by a black note can also be named as sharps or flats.

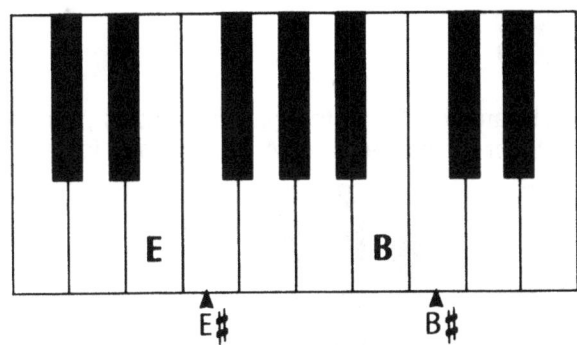
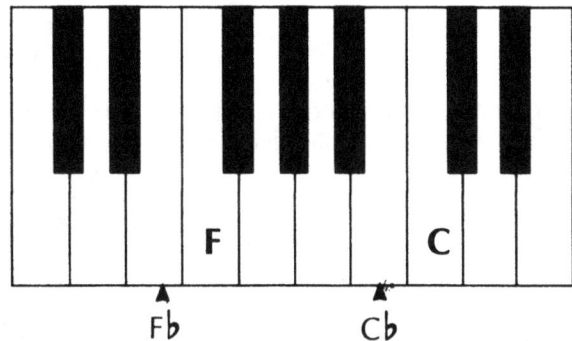

ENHARMONIC CHANGE

The practice of naming the same key in two or more different ways is called Enharmonic Change.
By using all of the note names available you can see that there are two names for every black note.

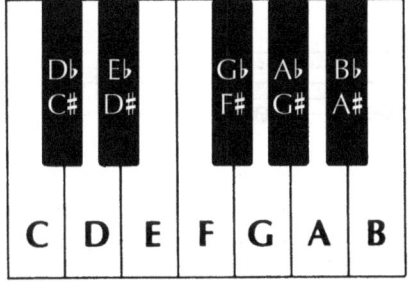

DOUBLE SHARP ✘ AND DOUBLE FLAT ♭♭

The sign used to raise a note by two semitones (a whole tone) is the Double Sharp sign. (✘)
The sign used to lower a note by two semitones is a Double Flat sign. (♭♭)
Therefore the note 'D' can be written as C Double Sharp (C✘) OR it can be written as E Double Flat. (E♭♭).
Thus each white note can also be written two or more ways.

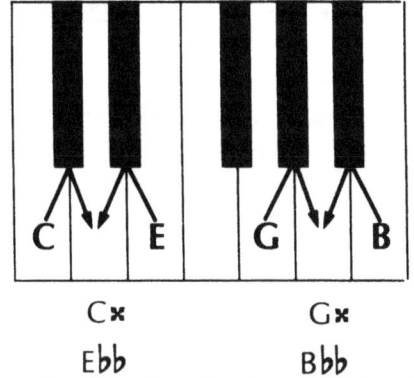

EXERCISE

Write in the name of the note and darken the correct black key or shade the correct white key.

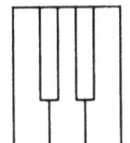 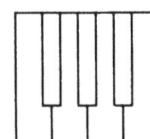 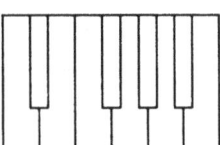 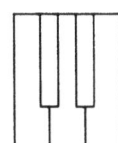 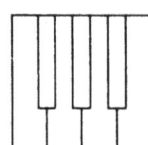 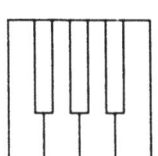

LESSON THIRTY

MORE ON SEMITONES AND WHOLE TONES

As mentioned in Lesson 26, a Semitone is the distance from one note to the very next nearest, and a Whole tone is therefore twice this distance (Semi meaning half). To play a whole tone miss out one key only.

EXERCISES

(1) Indicate the distances on the second octave of the keyboard, of the notes that the arrows point to. Follow the example given in the lower octave. Write S for Semitone and W for Whole Tone.

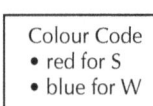

Colour Code
• red for S
• blue for W

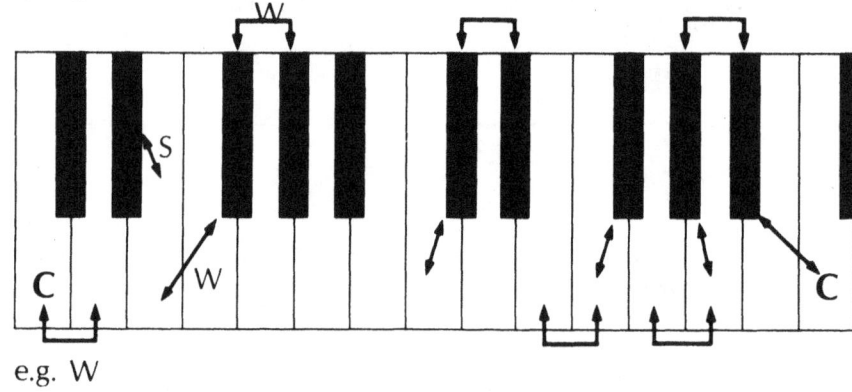

e.g. W

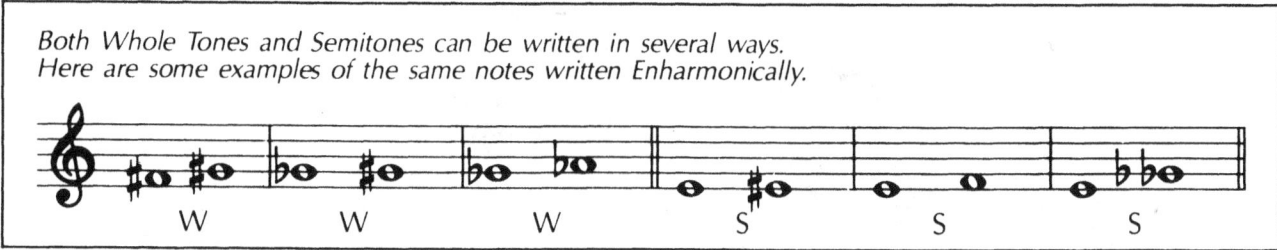

Both Whole Tones and Semitones can be written in several ways.
Here are some examples of the same notes written Enharmonically.

In the next exercise, The Tones and Semitones are all written as Steps or Seconds. I have done this so that this topic will lead logically to the topic of Scale construction, where all notes are written in Seconds from each other.

(2) Indicate whether the following notes are moving by Whole Step or Half Step (Semitone). Use W and S. Notice the Clef.

(3) Write the second note of each pair, a Whole Tone or Semitone **higher** than the given note. For the purpose of this exercise write the your note a Second higher than the given note, then adjust the Sharps or Flats to suit.

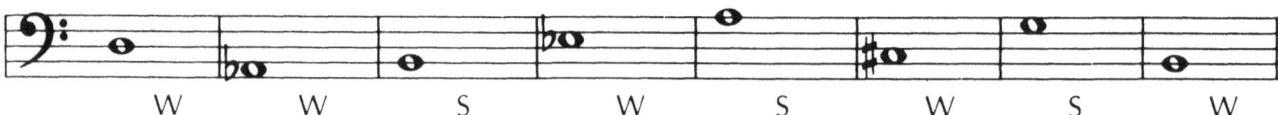

(4) Write the second note of each pair, either a Whole Tone or a Semitone **lower** than the given note.

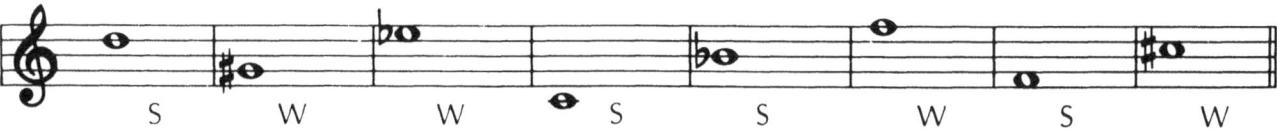

LESSON THIRTY-ONE

MAJOR SCALE

The word Scale comes from the Italian word 'scala' meaning ladder. A scale consists of a series of notes in succession.
There are several types of scales each with its own combination of tones and semitones.
The MAJOR SCALE is the most commonly used scale in music from the Seventeenth Century forward.

> The MAJOR SCALE PATTERN consists of Whole Tones and Semitones in the following order.
> **W W S W W W S**. (That is: two tones followed by a semitone and then three tones followed by a semitone.)

If this pattern is begun on C on the keyboard the following notes will all be white notes. C Major Scale is the only all white note Major scale on the keyboard. The dots and curved lines on the keyboard itself give the 'pathway' of the scale.

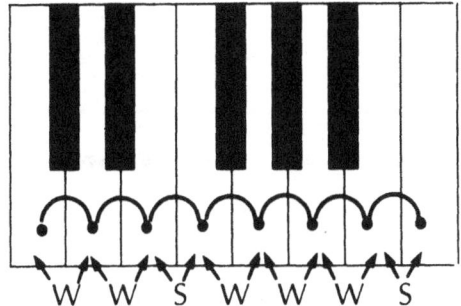
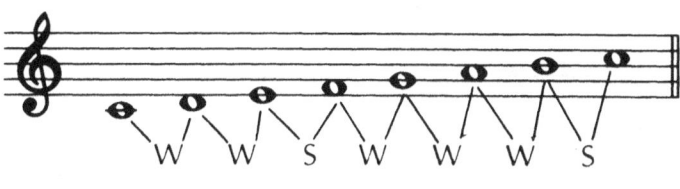

If the pattern is begun on G, the Black note F sharp will need to be used to that the notes conform to the pattern.

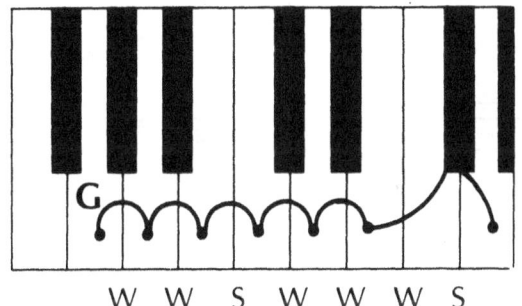
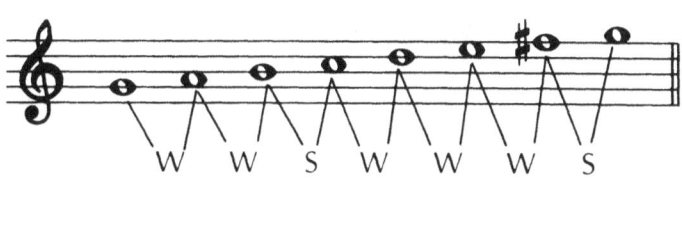

Here is the Major scale pattern and keyboard pathway for E♭ Major scale, as well as the scale in written form. Notice the clef.

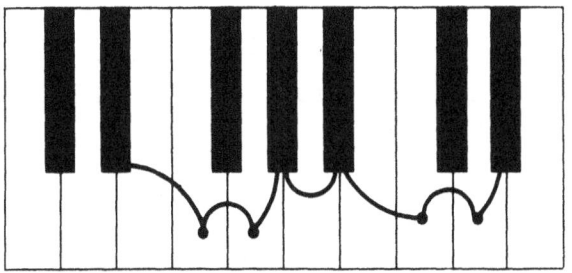

> ### THE KEY SIGNATURE
> When a scale is built using the Major Scale Pattern, the number of sharps or flats which appear become the SIGN of the scale or key — the 'Key Signature'.
> For instance, the Key Signature for C Major scale is **no** sharps or flats, while the Key Signature for G Major scale is **one sharp** (F♯) and the Key Signature for E flat Major is **three flats** (B♭, E♭ and A♭).

LESSON THIRTY-TWO

MORE ON KEY SIGNATURES

Once the scale has been written according to the Major scale pattern, the Sharps or Flats can be collected together and written at the beginning of the Stave. The resulting shape of the bunch of sharps or flats forms a definite recognisable unit or 'sign'.

When all the Sharps or Flats are written at the beginning of a piece of music, all the notes with the same letter name as the sharps or flats in the Key Signature must be played sharp or flat as the case may be, no matter which clef or area (register) of the instrument is being used.

Here are the Key-Signatures for G Major Scale and E♭ Major Scale in both Treble and Bass Clefs.

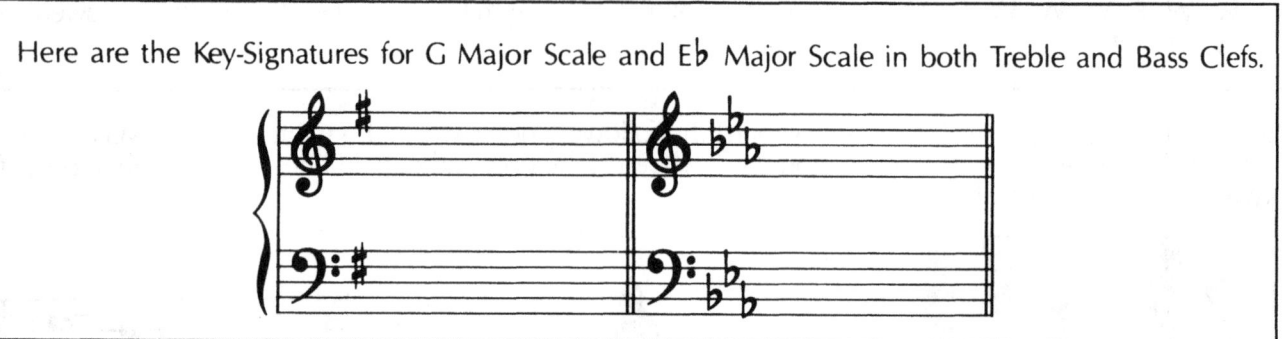

EXERCISES

(1) Find the keyboard pathway for D Major scale by placing a dot on each scale note and joining the dots with curved lines. Follow the Major scale pattern of W W S W W W S.
Next adjust the sharps on the WRITTEN scale to agree with the keyboard pathway. Remember that scales generally use notes in alphabetical order, so there must be one note of each letter name in each scale. (The same Major scale would not have both F Natural and F Sharp in it).

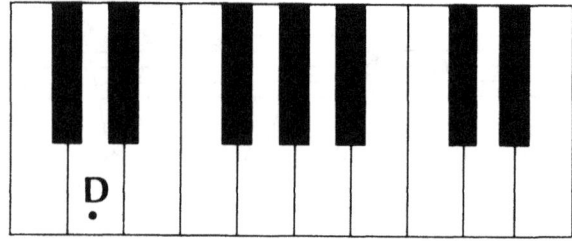 

(2) Find the keyboard pathway for F Major Scale. Adjust the written scale to agree with the pathway. You will find that F Major scale needs to have one note flattened.

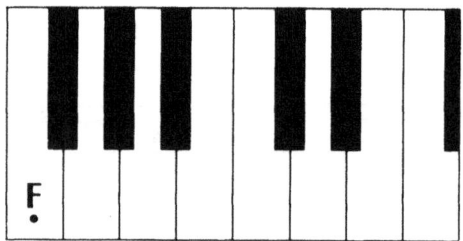 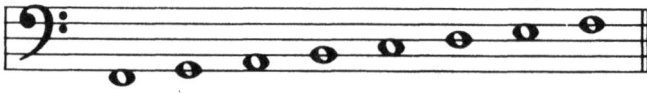

(3) Find the keyboard pathway for B Flat Major scale then adjust the written scale to agree with the pathway.

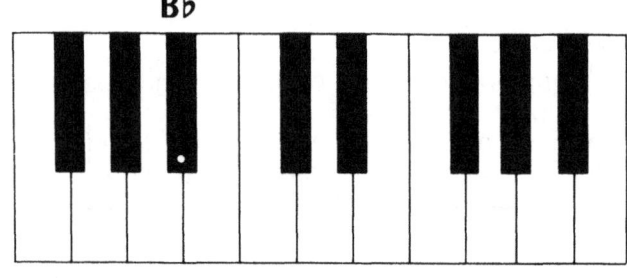 

LESSON THIRTY-THREE

The NATURAL SIGN ♮
A Natural Sign cancels a sharp or a flat, bringing the note back to the original white note on the keyboard.

ACCIDENTALS
A ♯, ♭ or ♮ which occurs in the body of a piece is called an **accidental**. Accidentals affect only the note in front of which they are placed and continue to affect that same note until the end of the bar in which it is used.

The bar line acts as an eraser cancelling the effect of the accidental.

For instance: in the key of C, the note F sharp would be an accidental.

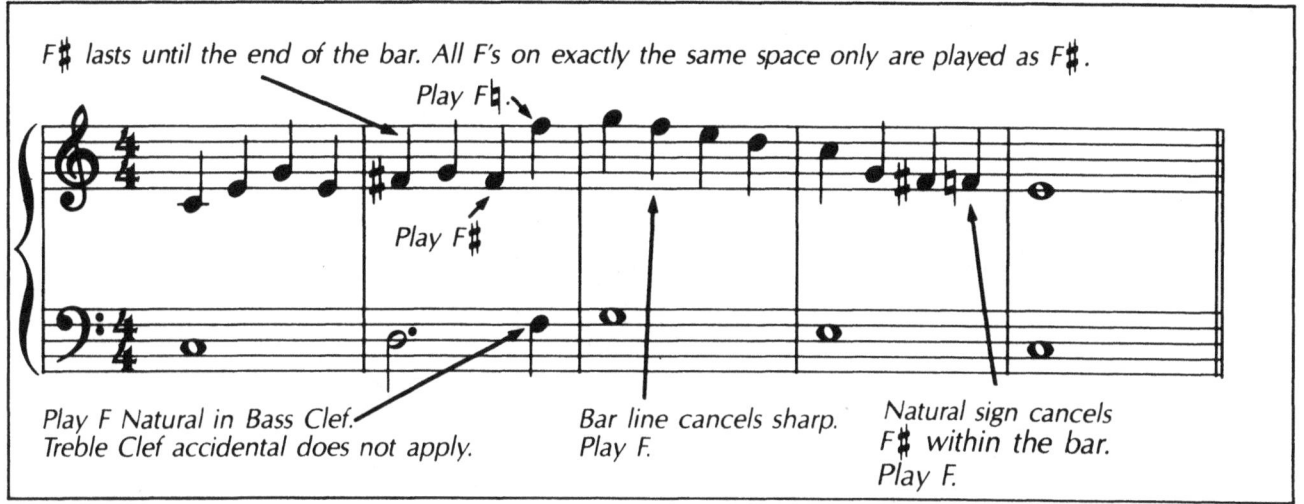

KEY SIGNATURE
As mentioned earlier, the key signature indicates that all notes in all registers with the same name as the sharps or flats in the key signature are to be played sharp or flat as the case may be.

An accidental will cancel a key signature sharp or flat for the duration of the bar, but only on the exact line or space on which it is written. The key signature sharp or flat will return again either through being written in again in the bar, or after a bar line has cancelled the accidental.

For instance: in the key of E Flat, the note B Natural would be an accidental.

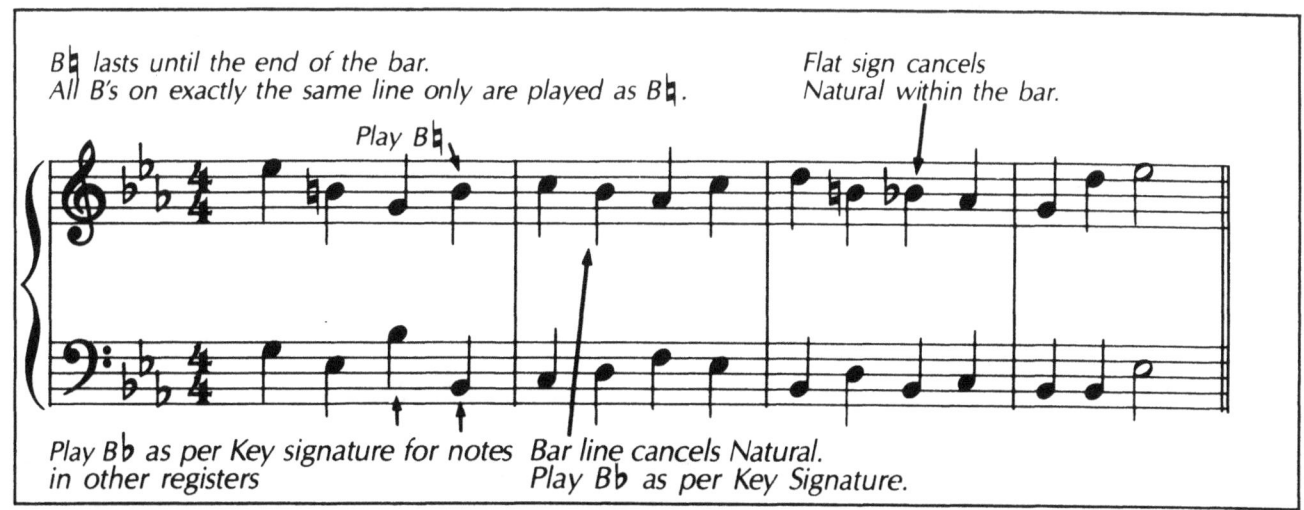

LESSON THIRTY-FOUR

EXERCISES

Darken the correct Black key or shade the correct White key for the following examples.
Note that the Key Signature is written before the Time Signature.
Refer to the keyboard pathways for D major and B♭ major scales that you have drawn in Lesson 32.

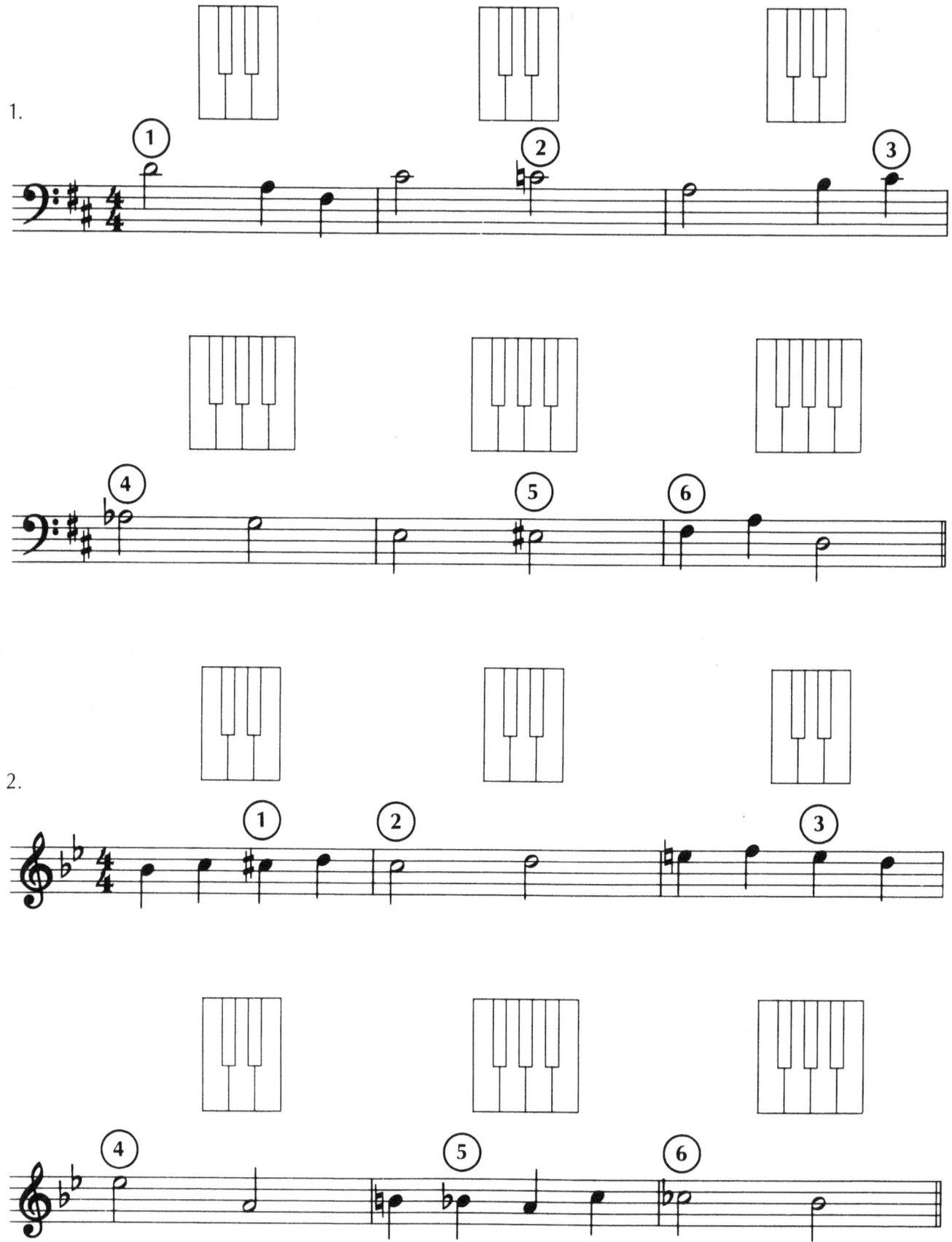

LESSON THIRTY-FIVE

TEST YOUR KNOWLEDGE

Fill in the blanks.

1. A .... has five lines and four spaces.

2. The distance between two notes is an ....

3. The Treble Clef is also known as the .... Clef.

4. A one-count note is known as a .... or ....

5. ▬ is a ....

6. A .... raises a note by a semitone.

7. A step can be written from a line note to a .... note.

8. W W S W W W S is the pattern for the ....

9. The top number in the time-signature tells .... counts in the bar.

10. The distance from one note to the very next nearest on the keyboard is called a ....

11. The .... Clef is used for both Alto and Tenor Clefs.

12. [staff notation] is the distance of a ....

13. ♭ is a .... Sign which .... a note by a semitone.

14. In Simple Time the Beat Note can be divided into .... equal parts.

15. Skips (3rds) and Jumps (5ths) are written from:

    .... note to .... note; or .... note to .... note.

16. The 4 in the 3/4 time signature stands for a ....

17. A .... rest can be used as a whole bar rest in any time-signature.

18. Another name for the F Clef is the .... Clef.

19. A .... cancels a sharp or a flat.

20. A .... is twice the distance of a semitone.

21. The name of the note which is a Skip (3rd) up from F is ....

22. [staff notation] This note is ....

23. Low C in the Bass Clef is written on the .... space.

24. [staff notation] is a ....

Lesson One: Q.2 L S L S S L L

Lesson Two: Q.1

Q.2

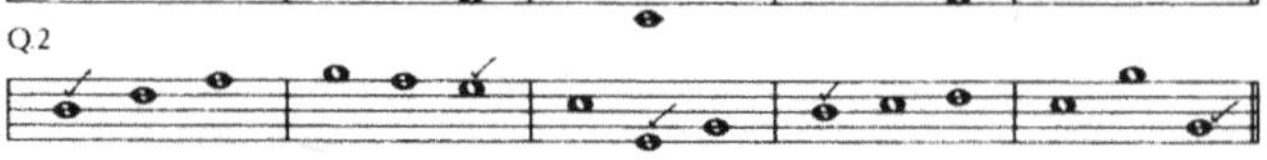

Q.3 HLLSLHSHLS

Lesson Four: Q.1

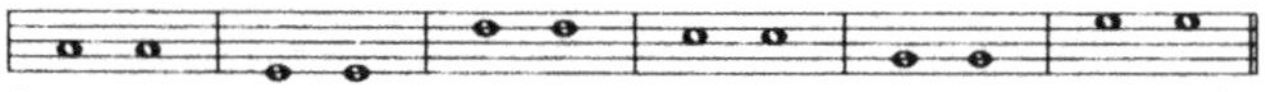

Q.2

Q.3

Q.4

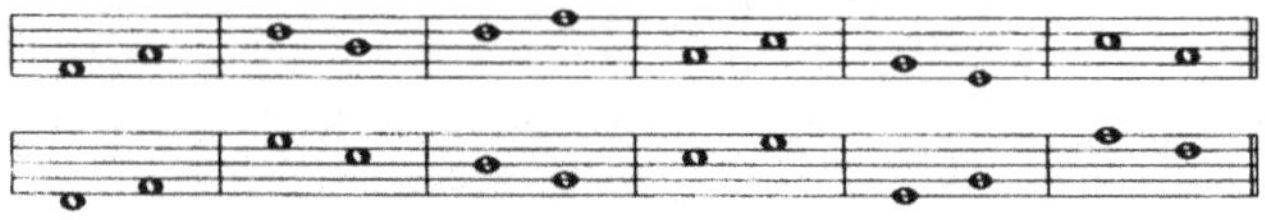

Q.5 S St↓ Sk↑ Sk↓ S St↑ Sk↑ S St↓ Sk↓

Lesson Six: Q.1 Sk+1 (4th)↓ J(5th)↑ J↓ Sk+1↑ J↑ Sk+1↓

Q.2 Sk↓ J↑ S St↑ Sk+1↓ J↓

Q.3

Q.4

Q.5

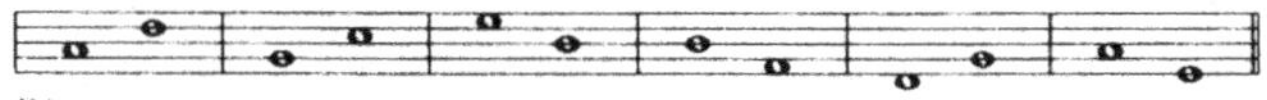

Q.6

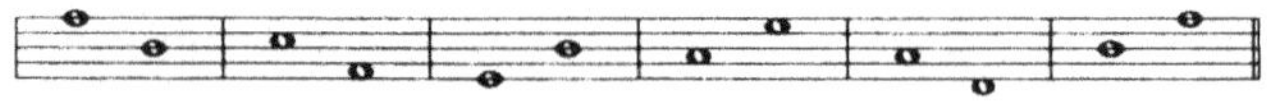

Lesson Seven: Q.1

Q.2

Q.3

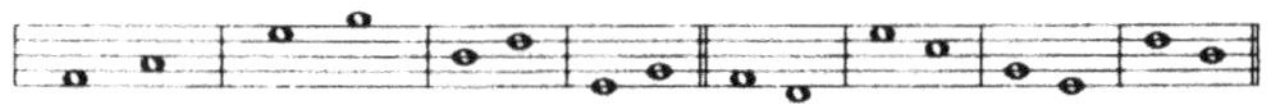

Q.4

Q.5

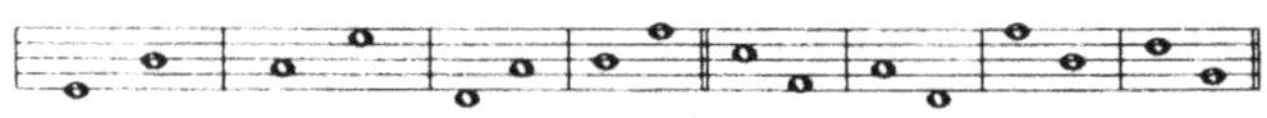

Lesson Eight: Refer to Keyboard at top of page.

Lesson Nine: 1. Bass Clef 2. C Clef 3. Treble Clef

Lesson Eleven: Q.1

St St Sk St Sk St — Sk Sk Sk St Sk Sk

D E G F D C — E C A B D F

Q2

St Sk St St Sk St Sk

↑D ↑F ↑G ↑A ↑C ↓B ↑D

Lesson Twelve: Q.1

Sk St Sk St J — St Sk Sk+1 St Sk+1

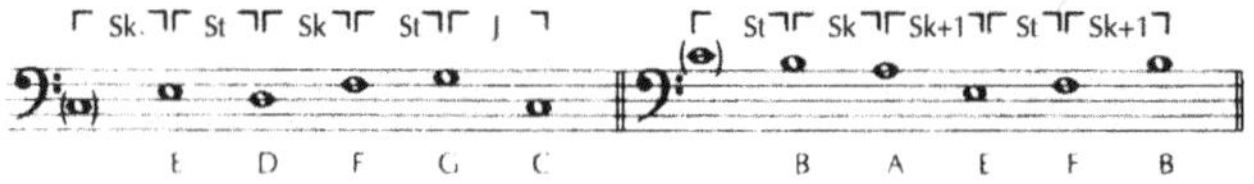

E D F G C — B A E F B

Q.2

Sk+1 Sk St Sk+1 St Sk+1

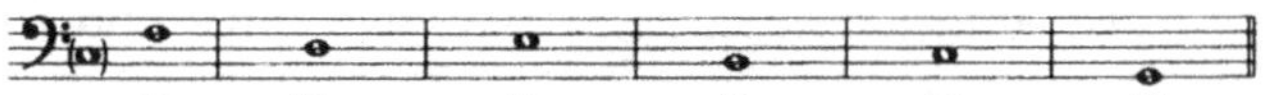

↑F ↓D ↑E ↓B ↑C ↓G

Q.3

Sk Sk St Sk J Sk+1

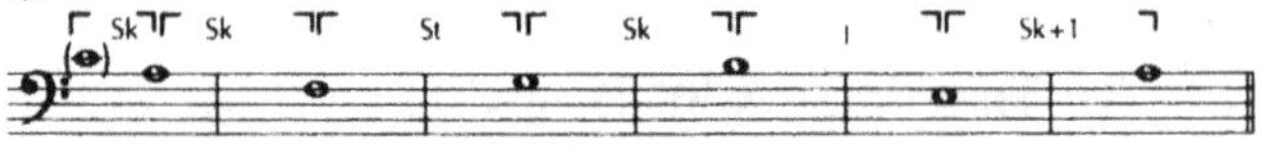

↓A ↓F ↑G ↑B ↓E ↑A

Lesson Thirteen: Q.1 ALTO CLEF

Sk St Sk St St Sk St Sk

C E F D C B G A C

Q.2 TENOR CLEF

Sk+1 St Sk J St Sk Sk+1 J

C G F A E D B F C

Q.3 ALTO CLEF — TENOR CLEF

Sk J Sk+1 — Sk+1 St Sk+1

MIDDLE C E↑ A↓ D↑ MIDDLE C G↓ F↓ B↑

Lesson Fourteen: Q.1 C F A C E G B C. C D F A C E G
Q.2 C G B D F A C. C E G B D F

Lesson Fifteen: Q.1 Treble Clef. C E D F E B C A E D G B C
Bass Clef C G B D A E G C F B G D C

Q.2

Sk Sk Sk+1 Sk Sk St Sk+1

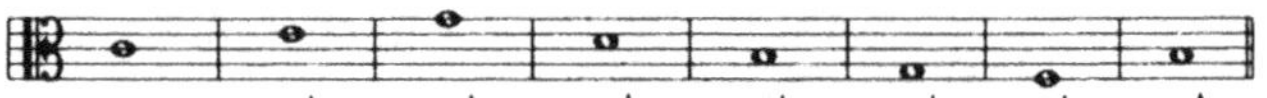

C F↑ G↑ D↓ B↓ G↓ F↓ B↑

Q.3 There are several choices for each note-name.

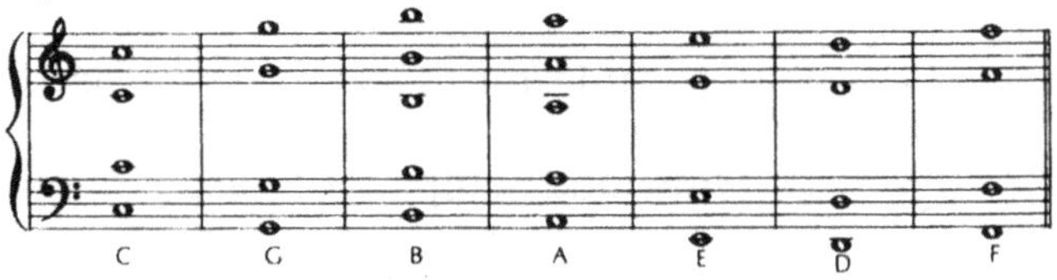

C G B A E D F

Q.4

Sk+1 St Sk Sk+1 Sk St J

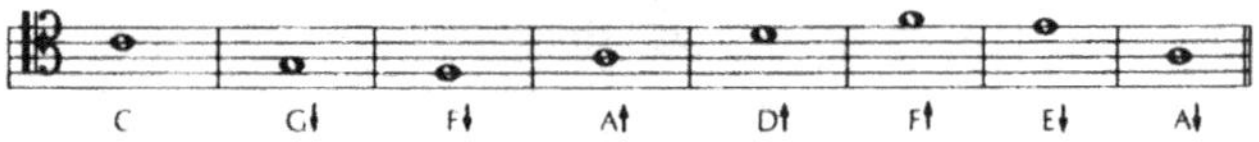

C G↓ F↓ A↑ D↑ F↑ E↓ A↑

Q.5 Alto: C G D G F C F Tenor: C G D F B F

Lesson Sixteen: 1. Whole Note or Semibreve. 2. Half Rest or Minim Rest. 3. Quarter Note or Crotchet 4. Eighth Rest or Quaver Rest. 5. Half Note or Minim. 6. Eighth Note or Quaver. 7. Whole Rest or Semibreve Rest. 8. Quarter Rest or Crotchet Rest.

Lesson Eighteen: (1) 2 1 3 2 4 4 ½ 1 ½ 1

(2) 

Lesson Nineteen: 6 2+1=3 1½ 4 1½ 3 6 3+1=4 3 1½+½=2

Lesson Twenty: 1. $3 \times \frac{1}{4} = \frac{3}{4}$ 2. $\frac{2}{2}$ 3. $\frac{4}{8}$ 4. $\frac{4}{2}$ 5. $\frac{3}{8}$ 6. $\frac{2}{4}$ 7. $\frac{2}{8}$ 8. $\frac{4}{4}$ 9. $\frac{3}{2}$

Lesson Twenty-Two: Q.1

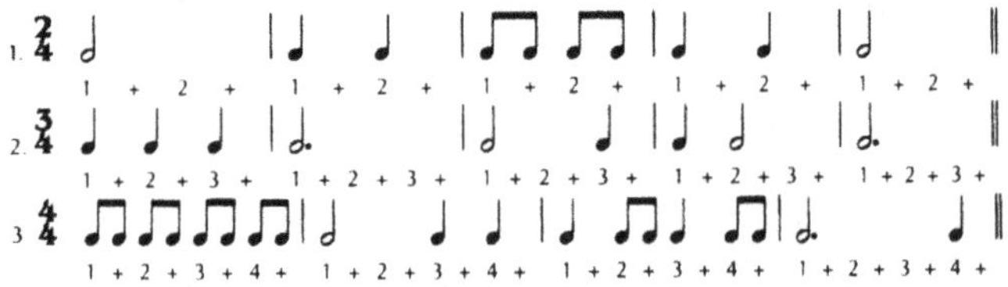

Q.2

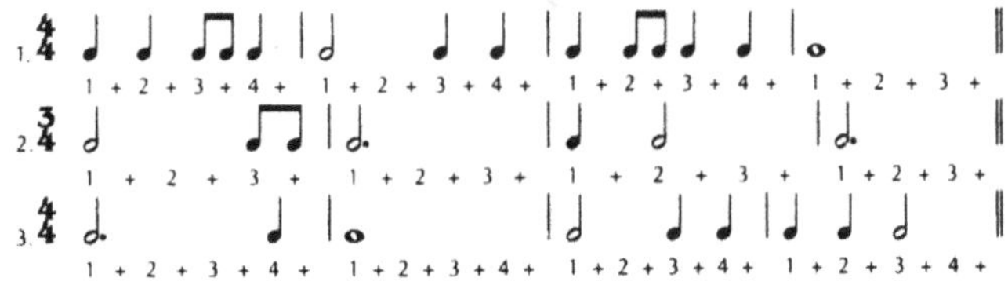

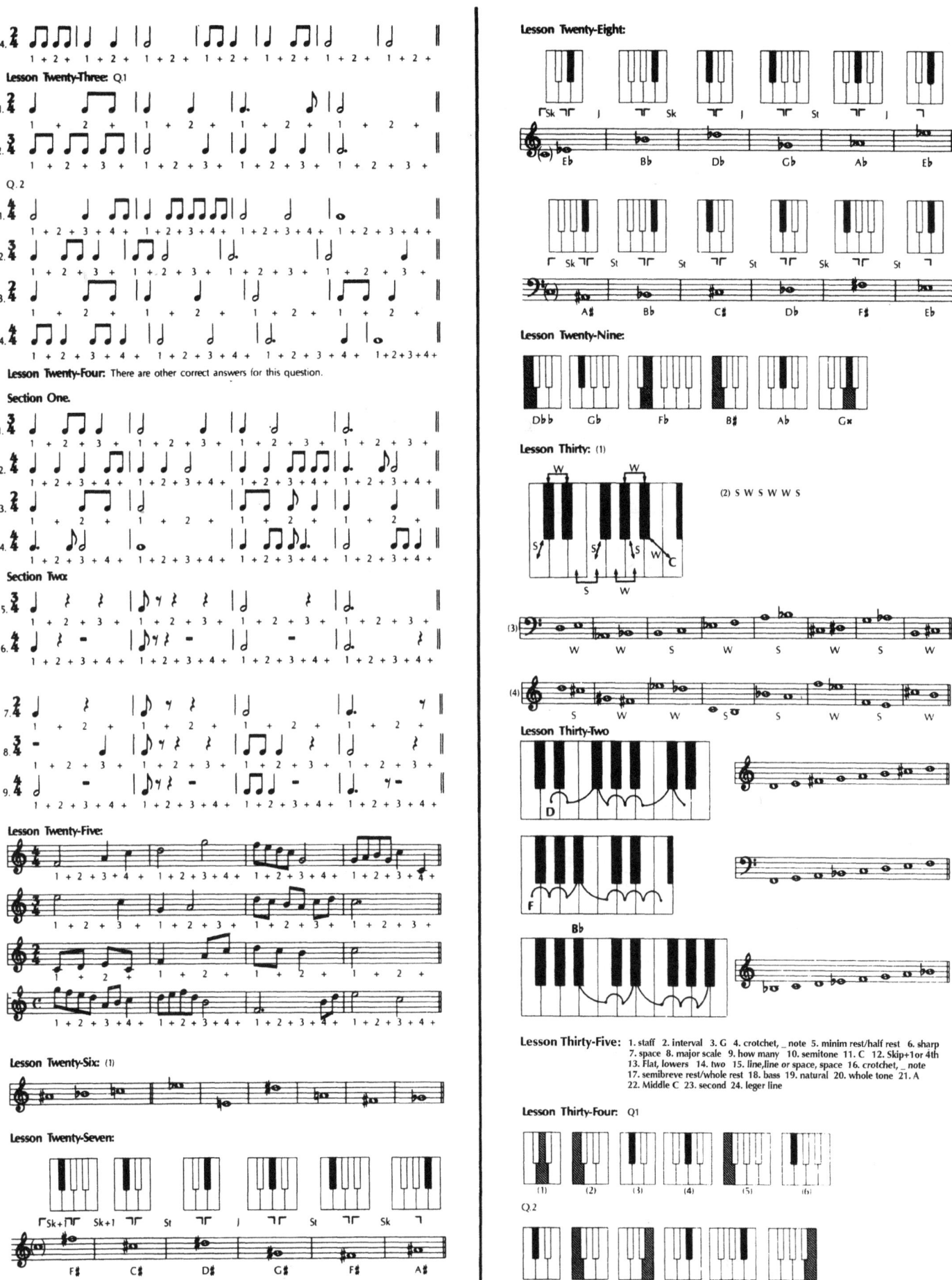

LESSON ONE

LARGER INTERVALS
Sixth — Seventh — Octave

In Book 1 the intervals from Prime (Unison) to Fifth were discussed.

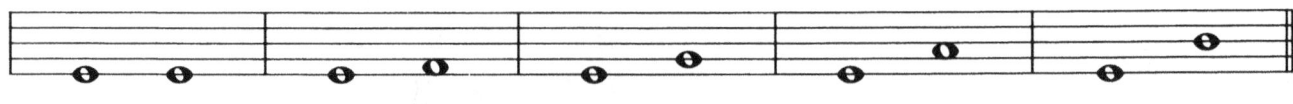

e.g. Prime (Unison)　　　2nd (Step)　　　3rd (Skip)　　　4th (Skip + 1)　　　5th (Jump)

The next three intervals to be learned are the SIXTH, SEVENTH and OCTAVE.

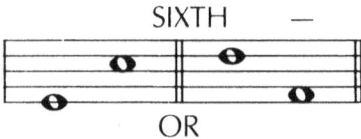

The **Sixth** is one step larger than the Fifth (Jump). It is always written from a Line Note to a Space Note or vice-versa. It looks similar to the Fourth (Skip-Plus-One) only wider apart.

The **Seventh** is two steps (a Skip or 3rd) larger than the Fifth. It is always written from a Space Note to another Space Note or from a Line Note to another Line Note. It looks like a larger version of the fifth.

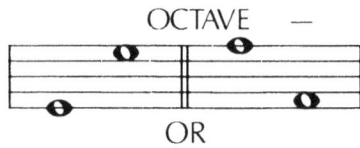

The **Octave** or **Eighth** is a step larger than the Seventh. It is written from a Line Note to a Space Note or vice-versa, similar to the Sixth and the Fourth. The names of the notes that make up the Octave distance are the same. That is C to C, or G to G. This is the reason that the interval of an Octave blends so well and sounds so pure. The word Octave is usually shortened to 8ve.

◆◆◆◆◆◆◆◆◆◆◆◆◆◆◆◆◆◆◆◆◆◆◆◆◆

EXERCISES

(1) Name the following intervals as 6th, 7th or 8ve.

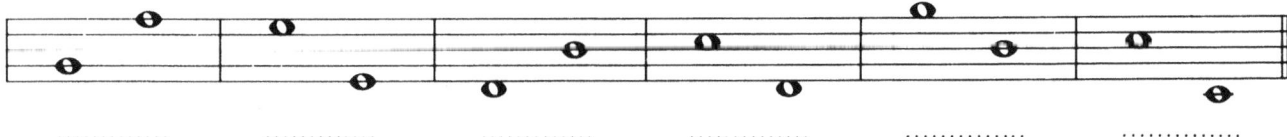

....　　　............　　　............　　　............　　　............　　　............

(2) Write the required intervals ABOVE the given notes.

7th　　　　6th　　　　8ve　　　　6th　　　　7th　　　　8ve

(3) Write the required intervals BELOW the given notes.

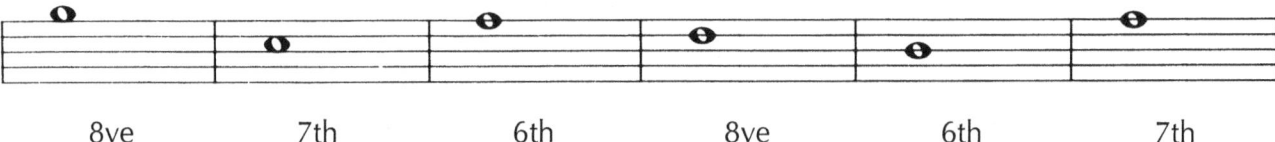

8ve　　　　7th　　　　6th　　　　8ve　　　　6th　　　　7th

42

LESSON TWO

HARMONIC AND MELODIC INTERVALS

Melodic Intervals — Intervals which are written with the notes **following** each other as in a Melody are known as **Melodic Intervals**.

Harmonic Intervals — Intervals in which the two notes are **sounded** at the **same time** are called **Harmonic Intervals**. A Harmonic Prime or 1st can occur when two different instruments play the same note. To write a Harmonic Prime, place the two notes as close together as possible.

INTERVAL FAMILIES

It is helpful when writing and reading intervals to think of them as falling into two families.

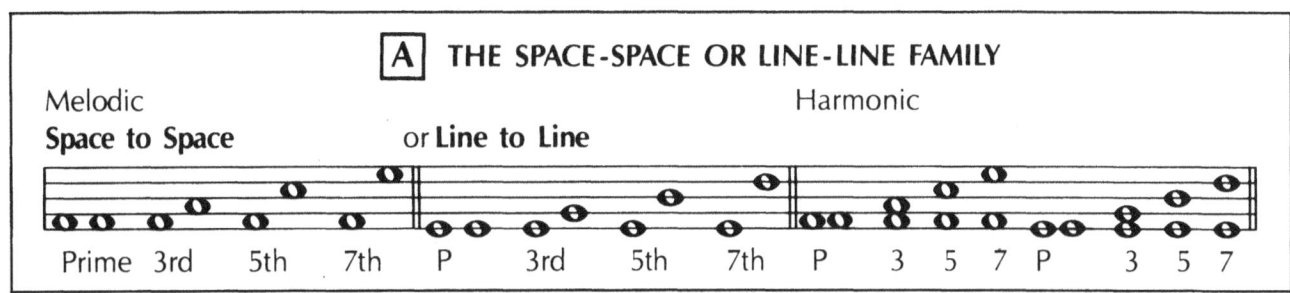

A — THE SPACE-SPACE OR LINE-LINE FAMILY

Melodic: Space to Space or Line to Line — Prime, 3rd, 5th, 7th, P, 3rd, 5th, 7th
Harmonic: P, 3, 5, 7, P, 3, 5, 7

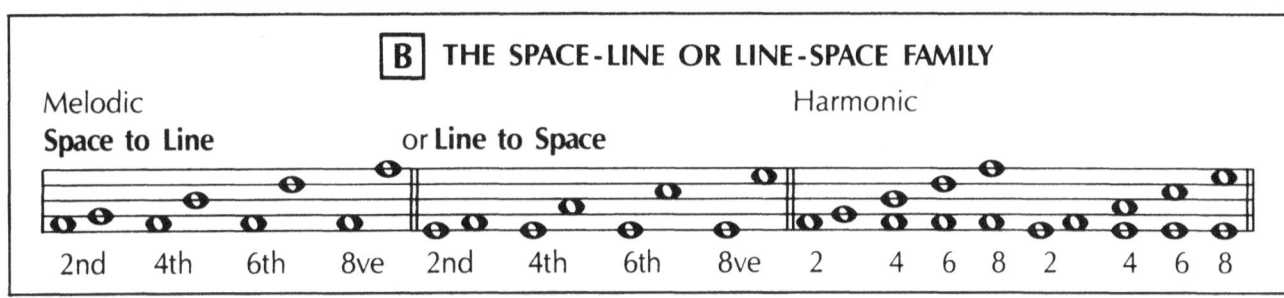

B — THE SPACE-LINE OR LINE-SPACE FAMILY

Melodic: Space to Line or Line to Space — 2nd, 4th, 6th, 8ve, 2nd, 4th, 6th, 8ve
Harmonic: 2, 4, 6, 8, 2, 4, 6, 8

Colour Code
- red for A
- blue for B

For further practice refer to the CTP

EXERCISES

(1) Name which family the following intervals belong to. A or B?

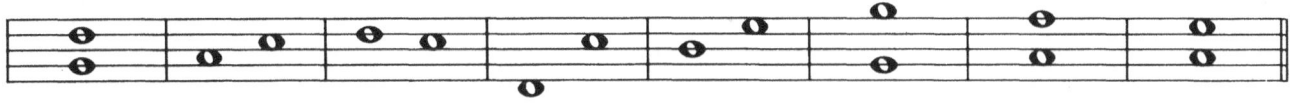

(2) Name the following intervals:

(3) Write these intervals above C as Harmonic Intervals.

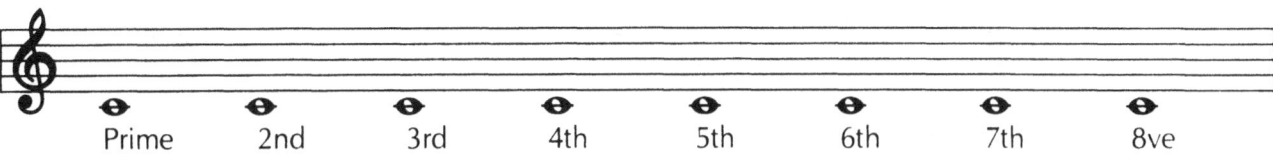

Prime   2nd   3rd   4th   5th   6th   7th   8ve

LESSON THREE

NOTE-NAMING ON THE GRAND STAFF AND TWO NEW SIGNPOST C's

(a) Here is a diagram of the location of VERY HIGH C and VERY LOW C on the Grand Staff. Notice that both C's are mirror image to each other written on the **second** Leger Line away from the staff.

(b) This diagram gives the location of **all** the Signpost C's covered up to this point in relation to the Grand Staff.

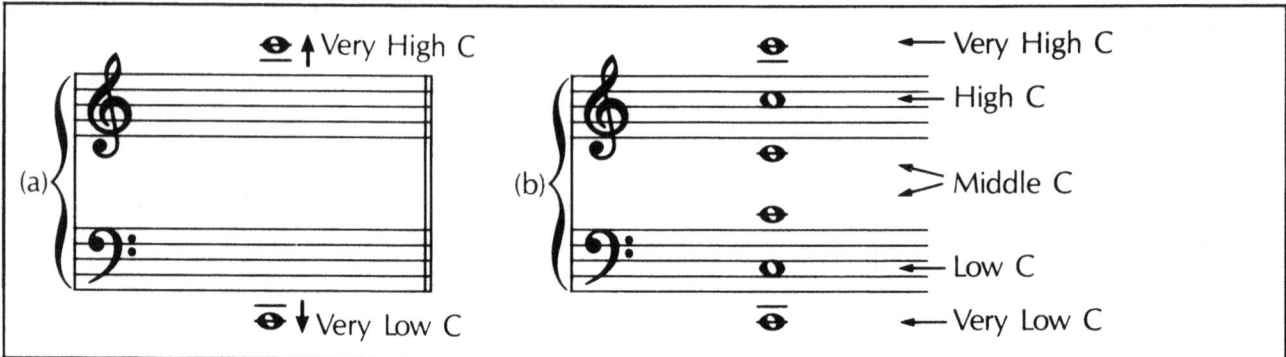

Presented below is the alphabetical list of note names which you can use to work out the names of the notes in the following questions.

I have given examples of how to work out the names of the notes in the intervals of a **Sixth**, **Seventh** and **Octave** using the alphabetical list.

◆◆◆◆◆◆◆◆◆◆◆◆◆◆◆◆◆◆◆◆◆◆◆◆◆◆◆◆◆◆

EXERCISES

(1) Use the method learned in Book 1 to write the intervals **above** the staff between the brackets. Then also use the system to figure out the note-name and write it in the space provided **under** the note. Take your bearings from the Signpost C's.

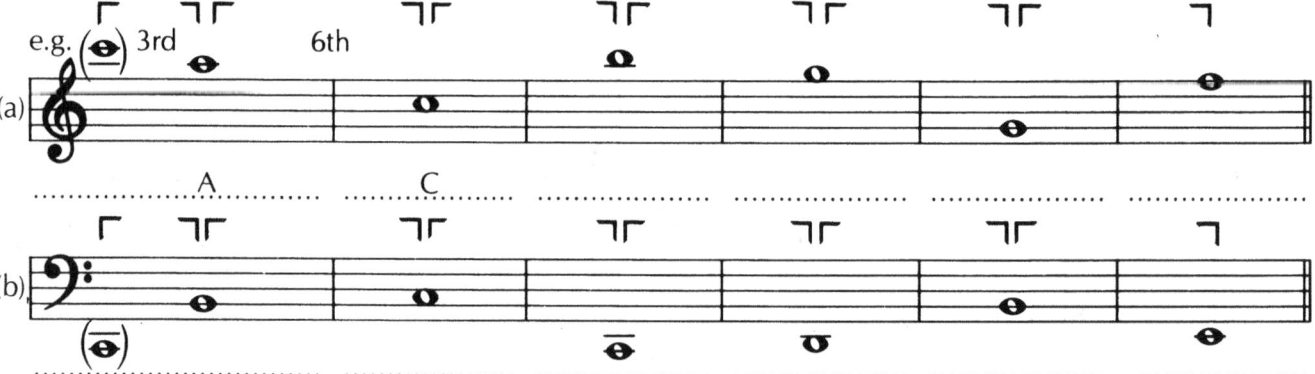

(2) (a) Work out the interval between each given letter name and write it above the staff.
    (b) Write the notes according to the size of each interval.

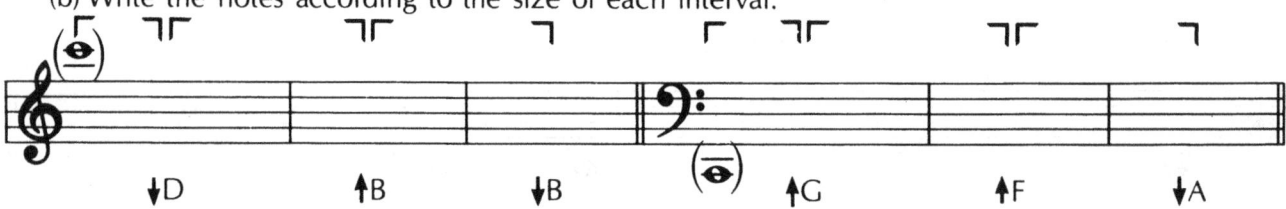

LESSON FOUR

MUSICAL TERMS INDICATING VOLUME

Italian has become the **international language** for indicating musical terms. Several Italian words are used to indicate volume.

Below is a list of these Italian Words, their abbreviations and their English meanings. They are listed from loud to soft.

ITALIAN WORD	ABBREVIATION	ENGLISH MEANING
Forte-Fortissimo	*fff*	very, very loud
Fortissimo	*ff*	very loud
Forte	*f*	loud
Mezzo Forte	*mf*	moderately loud
Mezzo Piano	*mp*	moderately soft
Piano	*p*	soft
Pianissimo	*pp*	very soft
Piano-Pianissimo	*ppp*	very, very soft

The suffix *'issimo'* means 'very'.
The word *Mezzo* means 'moderately'.

Several other words and signs are used to indicate a change in volume.

ITALIAN WORD	ABBREVIATION OR SIGN	ENGLISH MEANING
Crescendo	*Cresc.* or ⟨	gradually louder
(Decrescendo / Diminuendo)	*Decresc.* or ⟩ / *Dim.* or ⟩	gradually softer / gradually softer

EXERCISE

Complete these sentences.

1. *p* is short for .... which means ....

2. *Fortissimo* means ....

3. The sign for gradually louder is ....

4. The abbreviation for *Mezzo Piano* is ....

5. *Dim.* means to become ....

6. *fff* stands for .... which means..................................

7. The suffix *issimo* means ....

8. .... is the sign for both *Decrescendo* and *Diminuendo* (gradually softer).

LESSON FIVE

DEGREE NUMBERS AND DEGREE NAMES

When scales are written, each note in the scale can be given a number from One to Eight. These numbers are DEGREE NUMBERS and are usually written in Roman Numerals as follows:

I	II	III	IV	V	VI	VII	VIII
(1)	(2)	(3)	(4)	(5)	(6)	(7)	(8)

Each of the notes of the scale can also be given a DEGREE NAME or Technical Name, which tells us something about the function of that note in relation to the scale.

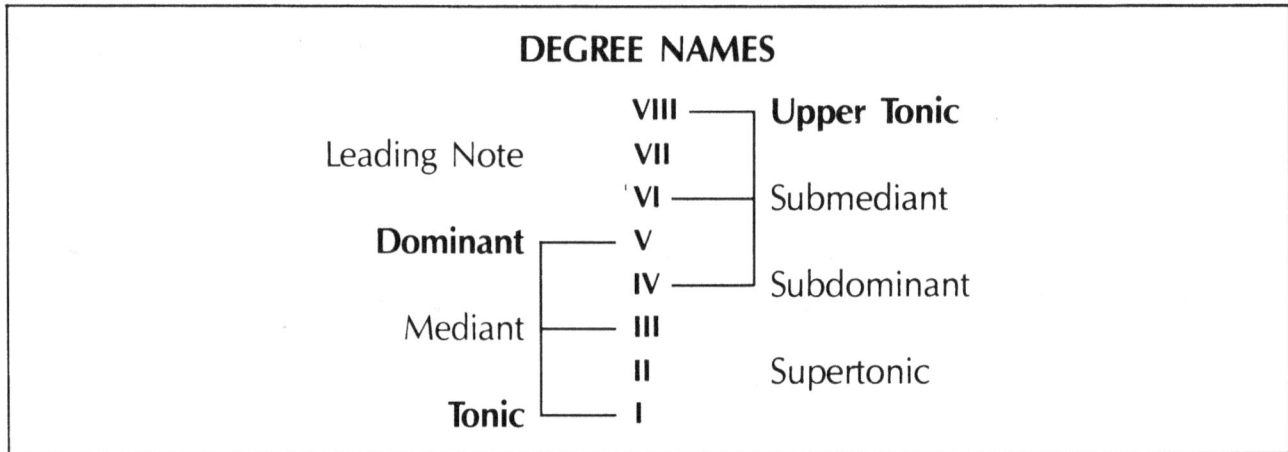

The first degree is called the TONIC — meaning keynote of the scale. The note an Octave above with the same name is called the UPPER TONIC.

The most important note in relation to the Tonic is the 5th degree of the scale — the DOMINANT.

The note which is the interval of a Fifth **below** the Upper Tonic is called the SUBDOMINANT or most important note below the Tonic. (*Sub means 'under'*)

Midway between the Tonic (I) and the Dominant (V) is the MEDIANT (III) meaning middle.

It follows then that the note that is **midway** between the Upper Tonic (VIII) and the Subdominant (IV) is the SUBMEDIANT (VI). (The middle note *under*).

The second degree (II) which is one bigger than the Tonic is known as the SUPERTONIC (*Super means 'bigger than'*).

The seventh degree (VII) is known as the LEADING NOTE (or Leading Tone) because of its function of leading the sound on to the Upper Tonic Note of the scale.

◆◆◆◆◆◆◆◆◆◆◆◆◆◆◆◆◆◆◆◆◆◆◆

EXERCISE

Fill in the blanks.

1. The Ist degree is called the ....

2. The Dominant is the .... degree.

3. The IIIrd degree is called the ....

4. The most important note **under** the Upper Tonic is the ....

5. The VIth degree is called the ....

6. The Supertonic is the .... degree.

7. The ....th or .... leads back to the Upper Tonic.

Special Note *Some texts use Roman numerals when referring to chords built on scale degrees and Arabic numbers topped with a caret (^) when referring to scale degrees used in a melody. For example: 5̂*

LESSON SIX

MAJOR SCALES AND MAJOR KEY SIGNATURES

When the Major scale pattern is used to build Major scales on every note on the keyboard, certain interesting features appear. The scales progress in a regular pattern; if the starting note of each scale is the interval of a **fifth** UP from the previous scale, then an extra **Sharp** is added to the previous sharps, or a Flat is deleted. If the starting note of each scale is a **fifth** DOWN from the Tonic of the previous scale, an extra **Flat** is added to the previous accidentals or a Sharp is deleted.

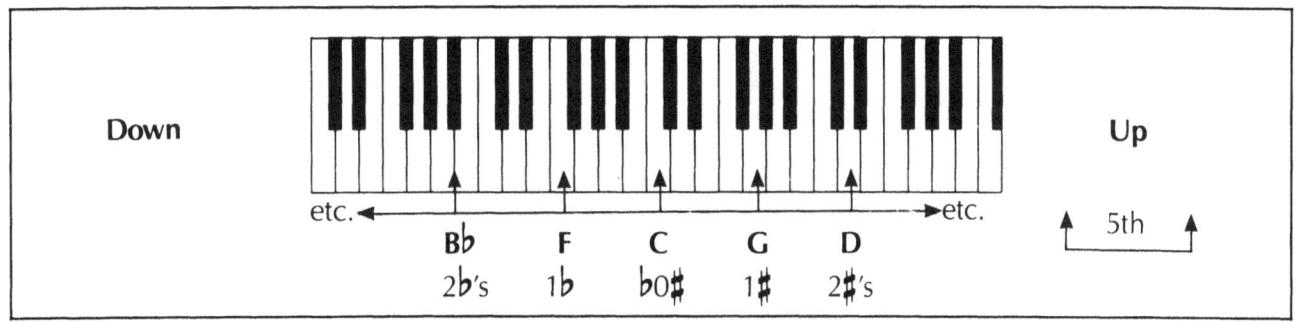

KEY SIGNATURE PATTERNS — SHARP KEYS

— The Sharps in the Key Signatures always follow the same regular pattern.
— The maximum number of sharps in a Key Signature is **seven**.
— The distance between each sharp in the Key Signature is always either a FIFTH up or in the inverted form — a Fourth down.)

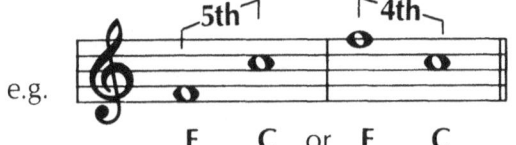

The order of sharps for a Key Signature with seven sharps is:

F C G D A E B

— The basic Key Signature pattern is created when the sharps move: 4th down, 5th up, 4th down, 5th up and so on (see the Mezzo Soprano Clef below).
— However when following this pattern in the Treble Clef, two of the sharps which would fall on Leger Lines above the staff, are dropped by an octave so that they fit on the staff. See the boxed sharps in the example below. The Treble Clef pattern is then matched by the pattern in the Bass Clef.
— In the Mezzo-Soprano Clef the true pattern appears, as all the sharps fall within the staff lines.

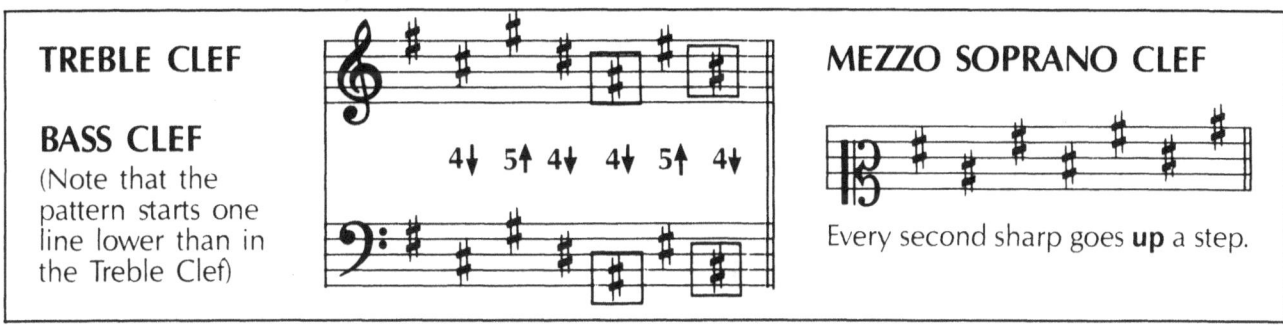

TREBLE CLEF

BASS CLEF
(Note that the pattern starts one line lower than in the Treble Clef)

MEZZO SOPRANO CLEF

Every second sharp goes **up** a step.

Some people use a rhyme to remember the order of sharps. Make up your own or learn this one:
Fat **C**ows **G**raze **D**own **A**t **E**aster **B**ay.

◆◆◆◆◆◆◆◆◆◆◆◆◆◆◆◆◆◆

EXERCISE

Write the seven Key Signature sharps in Treble, Bass and Mezzo Soprano Clefs (C Clef).

TREBLE   **BASS**   **MEZZO SOPRANO**

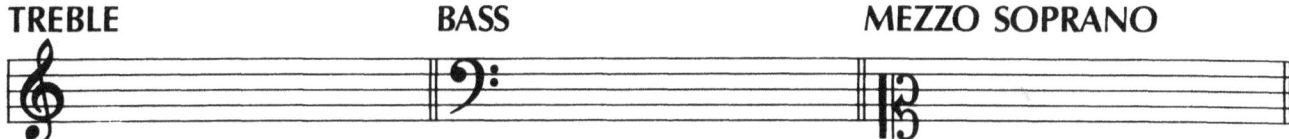

LESSON SEVEN

KEY SIGNATURE PATTERNS — FLAT KEYS

— The maximum number of flats in a Key Signature is **seven**.

— A Key Signature with seven flats would present the flats in this order:

B   E   A   D   G   C   F

— This is the order of the sharps in reverse (the rhyme backwards) or as you can see the word BEAD with G C F added on.

— Here is how the seven flat Key Signature looks in Treble, Bass and Tenor Clefs. Notice that each flat is either a **FIFTH** Down or a Fourth up from the next.

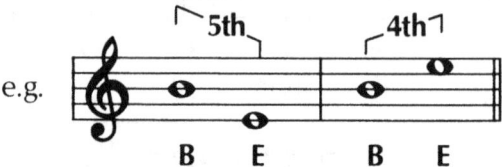

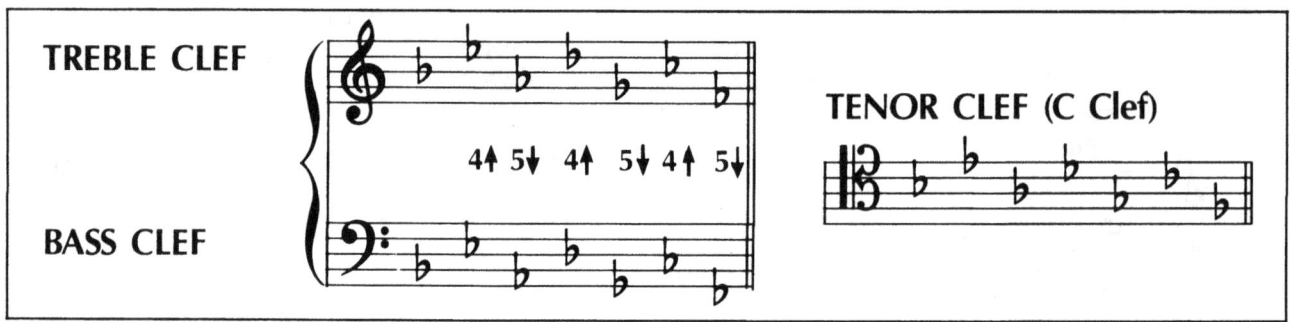

The regular look of the pattern can be maintained in the above Clefs as the Leger Lines are not encountered. Note that every second flat goes **down** a step.

◆◆◆◆◆◆◆◆◆◆◆◆◆◆◆◆◆◆◆◆◆◆◆

EXERCISES

(1) Write the seven flats of the Key Signature in Treble, Bass and Tenor Clefs.

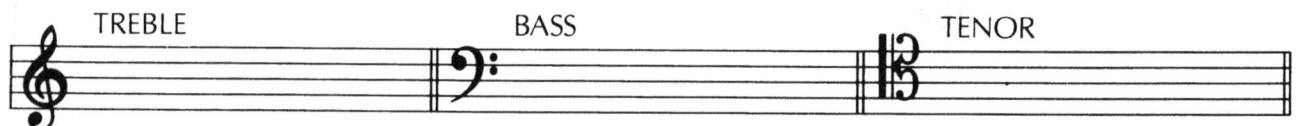

> IF A KEY SIGNATURE HAS LESS THAN SEVEN SHARPS OR FLATS, TAKE AS MANY AS NEEDED FROM THE SEQUENCE ALWAYS WORKING FROM THE VERY FIRST SHARP OR FLAT IN EACH SEQUENCE.
>
>
>
>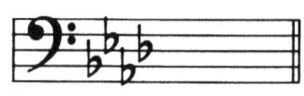

(2) Write the number of Sharps or Flats as required for these Key Signatures.

Two Flats   Five Sharps   Six Flats   Four Sharps

LESSON EIGHT

MAJOR SCALES
Scale Pattern and the Tetrachord

MAJOR SCALE PATTERN
Major Scales are all built using the same pattern of Whole Tones (T) and Semitones (S).

That is: **T T S T T T S**

TETRACHORD
The Major Scale pattern can be seen in another light, as two four-note groups each containing T T S and being connected by a Tone (T).

This four note group is known as a TETRACHORD from 'tetra' meaning 'four' and 'chord' meaning 'a group of notes'.

EXAMPLE

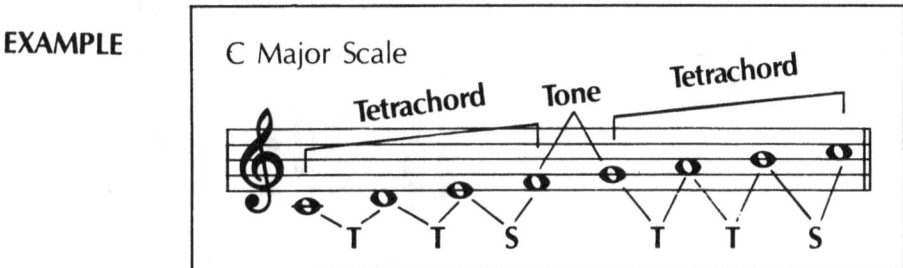

Notice that the second tetrachord for C Major Scale begins on the FIFTH note of the scale.

When you refer back to Lesson Six, you will recall that the manner in which the scales progress was discussed.

If the starting note for each scale is a **Fifth** UP from the previous scale, then an extra sharp is added to the Key Signature or a Flat is deleted.

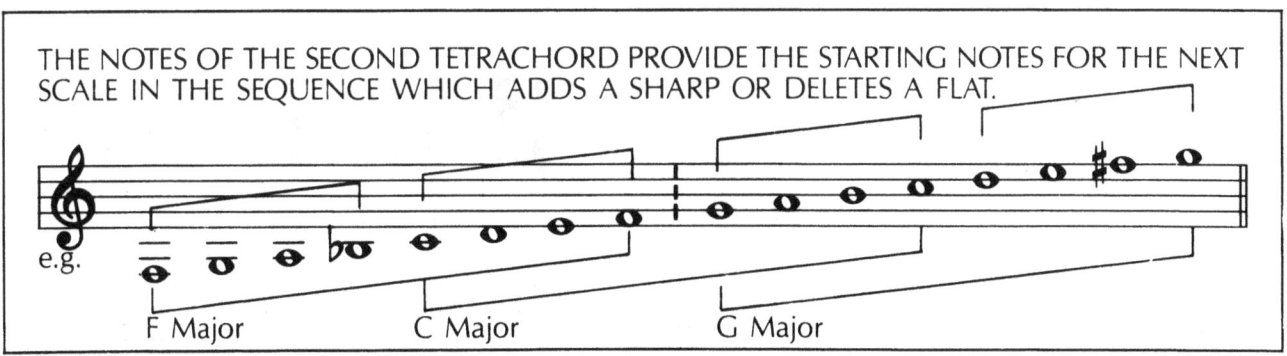

Use the Tetrachord as a means of checking your answers in the questions on the following pages.

LESSON NINE

MAJOR SCALES — SHARP KEYS
EXERCISE

Write out the Major Scales with sharps in the Key Signature, following the example given on this page and continuing on into the next page.

Below are the first three scales in the Cycle worked out from the point of view of the Major Scale pattern.

The starting note for each following scale is the FIFTH note of the previous scale.

The keyboard pattern has been worked out before the sharps have been added to the written scale.

After the scale has been written using accidentals, the number of sharps has been collected together to form a Key Signature. Refer to Lessons Six and Seven for the order in which the sharps should be written.

The fourth scale has been left for you to write out.

Place the letter-names of the scales in the boxes.

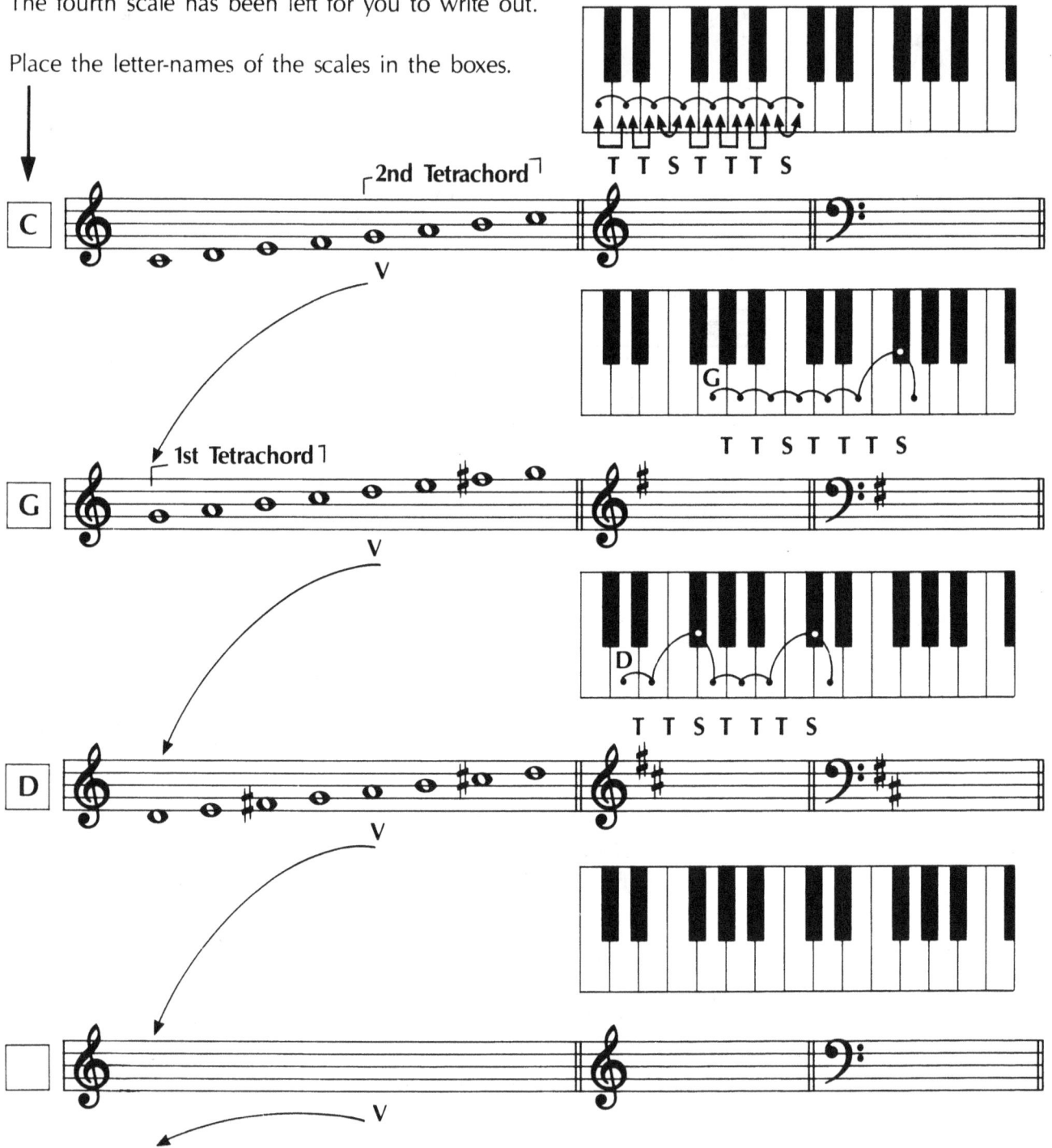

This is the starting note for the next Scale in the Cycle, to be written in Lesson Ten.

LESSON TEN

REMAINING MAJOR SCALES — SHARP KEYS

Work out the remaining Major scales in Sharp Keys by following the example given on the previous page. Work in five stages.

(1) Find the Fifth note of the previous scale to use as the Tonic Note of the next.

(2) Write a ladder of notes one octave in range, spacing out the notes on the staff so as to allow for any sharps to be written in front of the notes.

(3) Work out the Keyboard Pattern for the scale and adjust the sharps on the written scale to agree with the Keyboard Pattern.

(4) Collate the sharps together to write the Key Signature for the scale in both Treble and Bass Clefs. Refer to Lessons 6 and 7 for the order in which to write the Key Signature sharps.

(5) Check that the notes in the SECOND Tetrachord in the first scale are the same as the notes of the FIRST Tetrachord in the following scale.

Place the letter-names of the scales in the boxes.

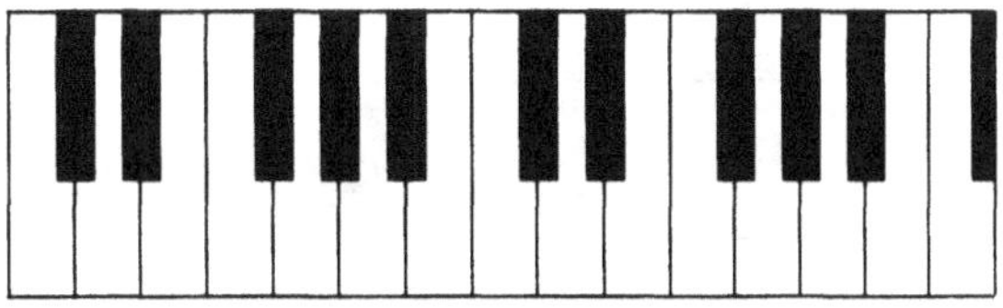

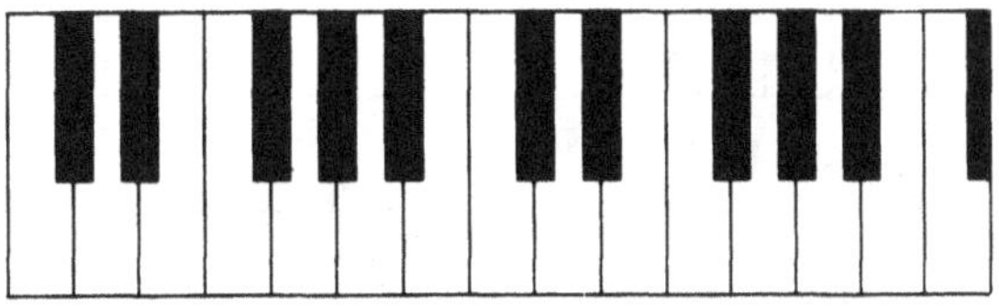

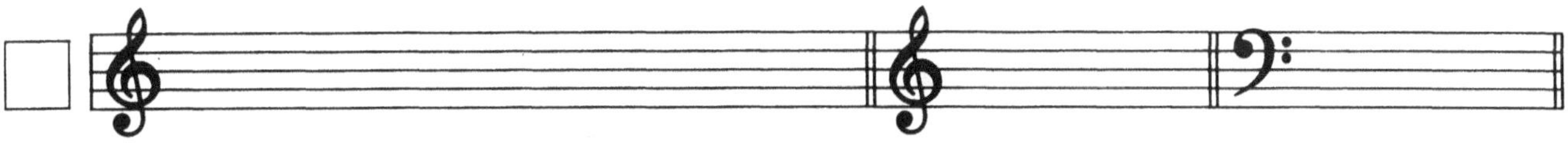

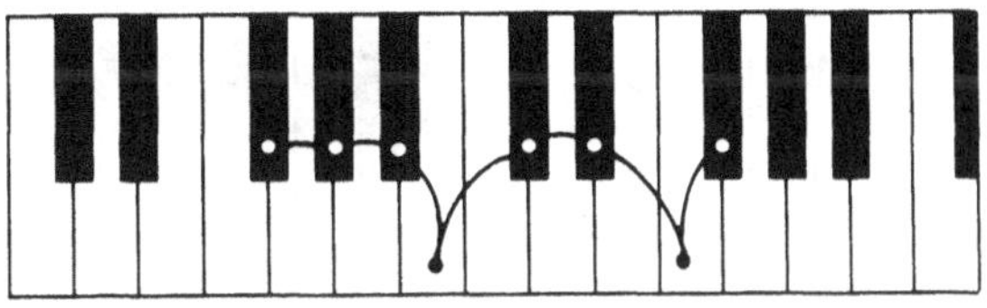

N.B. As this scale begins and ends on a black note with the same name, the sharp is counted once only, in the Key Signature.

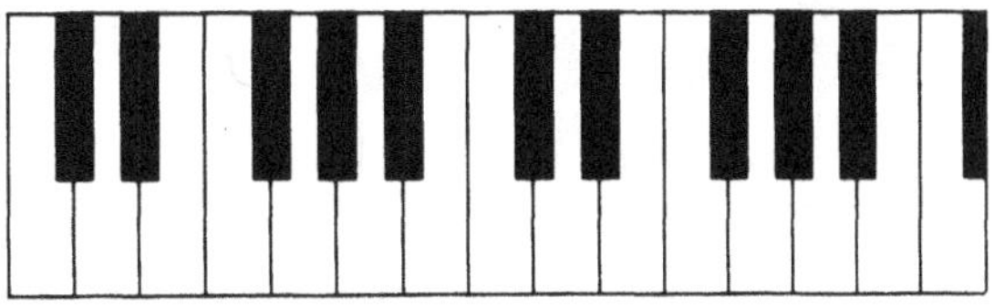

LESSON ELEVEN

MAJOR SCALES — FLAT KEYS

Using a similar method to the previous page, work out the scales which have FLATS in the Key Signature. The Keyboard Pattern can be worked out using the T T S T T T S formula.

However this time the starting note of the following scale is a FIFTH **lower** than the Upper Tonic of the scale and the FIRST Tetrachord of each scale becomes the SECOND Tetrachord of the next in the series.

FOLLOW THE EXAMPLE GIVEN TO COMPLETE THE SEVEN FLAT SCALES OVER THE NEXT TWO PAGES.

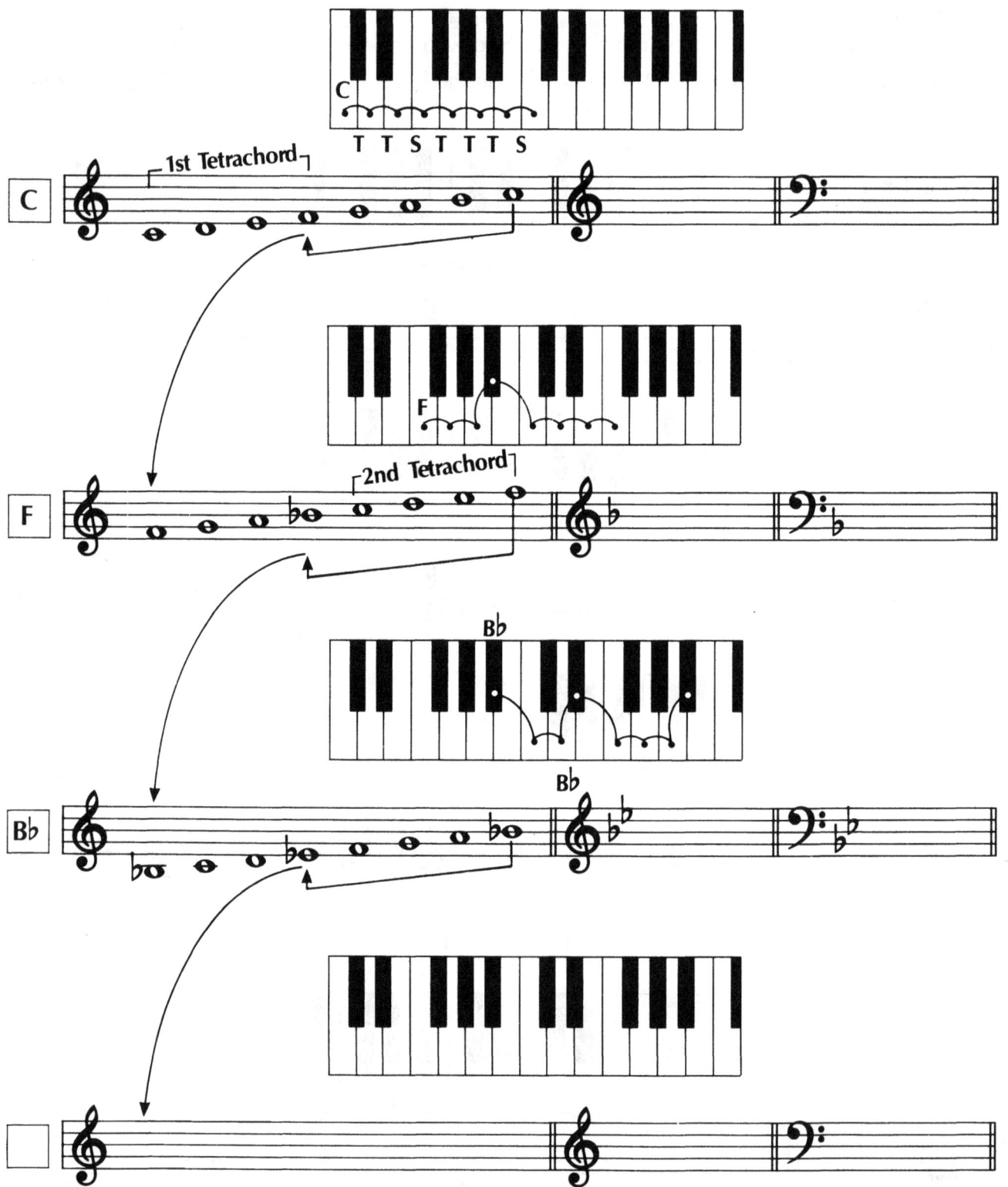

LESSON TWELVE

REMAINING MAJOR SCALES — FLAT KEYS

If you have worked out the fourth scale on the previous page correctly you will have found that the starting note for the next scale in the cycle is **A Flat.**

Begin this page with A Flat Scale and then work out the remaining Flat Key Signature scales.

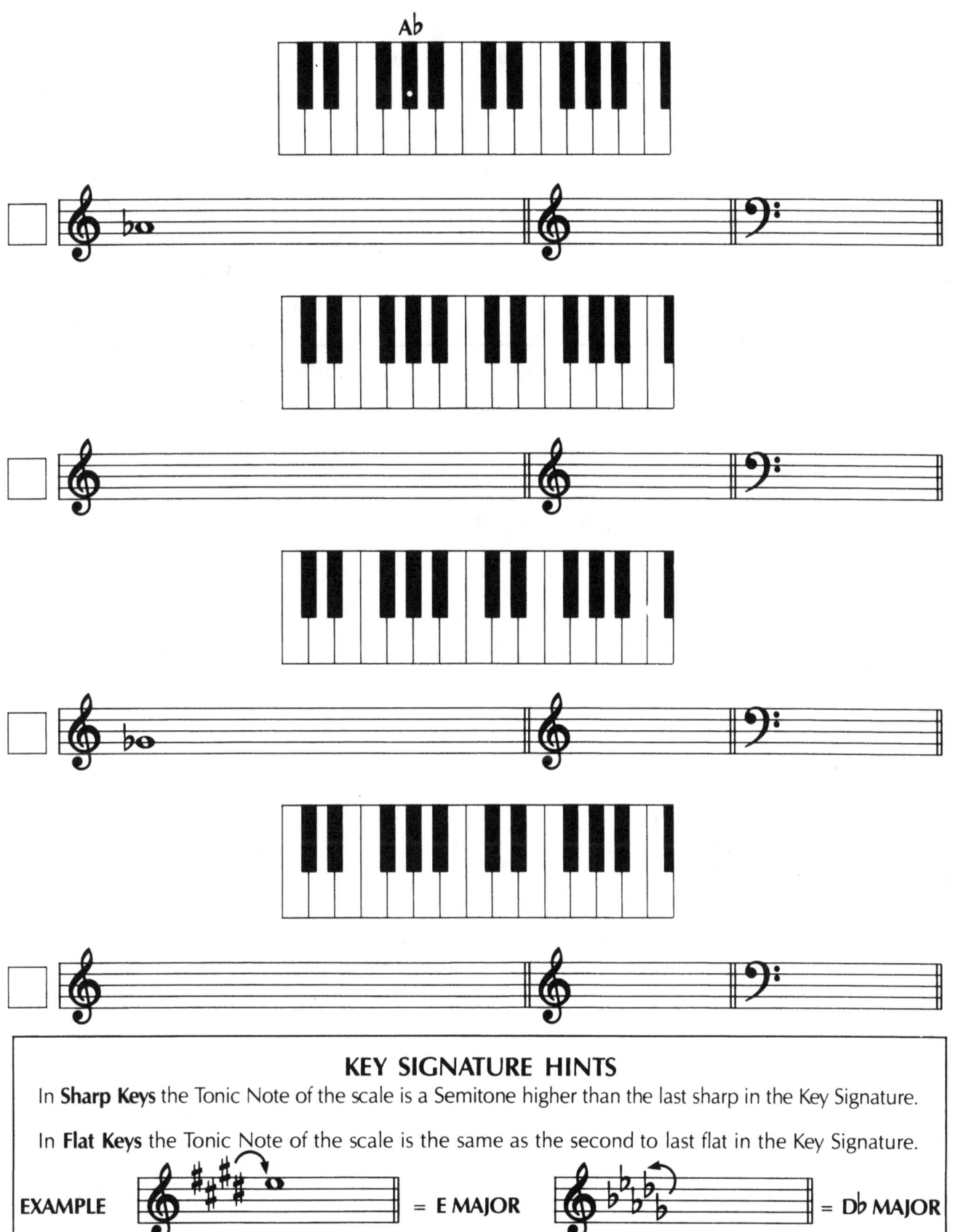

KEY SIGNATURE HINTS

In **Sharp Keys** the Tonic Note of the scale is a Semitone higher than the last sharp in the Key Signature.

In **Flat Keys** the Tonic Note of the scale is the same as the second to last flat in the Key Signature.

EXAMPLE = E MAJOR   = Db MAJOR

LESSON THIRTEEN

THE CIRCLE OR CYCLE OF FIFTHS

As you have seen on the previous pages, the connection between each scale and the scale with one more or one less sharp, is the distance (interval) of a FIFTH. If the pattern continues from one scale to the next, the cycle arrives back at the starting scale once again.

The easiest way to demonstrate this, is to lay the keys out in a circle, which is where the name CIRCLE OF FIFTHS comes from. The circle also reminds us of a clock, as at the Three O'Clock mark we find the scale with **three** sharps and at the Six O'Clock mark we find the scale with **six sharps**.

The sharp keys in ascending order of sharps are on the right of the circle and the flat keys in ascending order of flats are on the left of the circle.

The number of sharps or flats in each key is found on the inner circle.

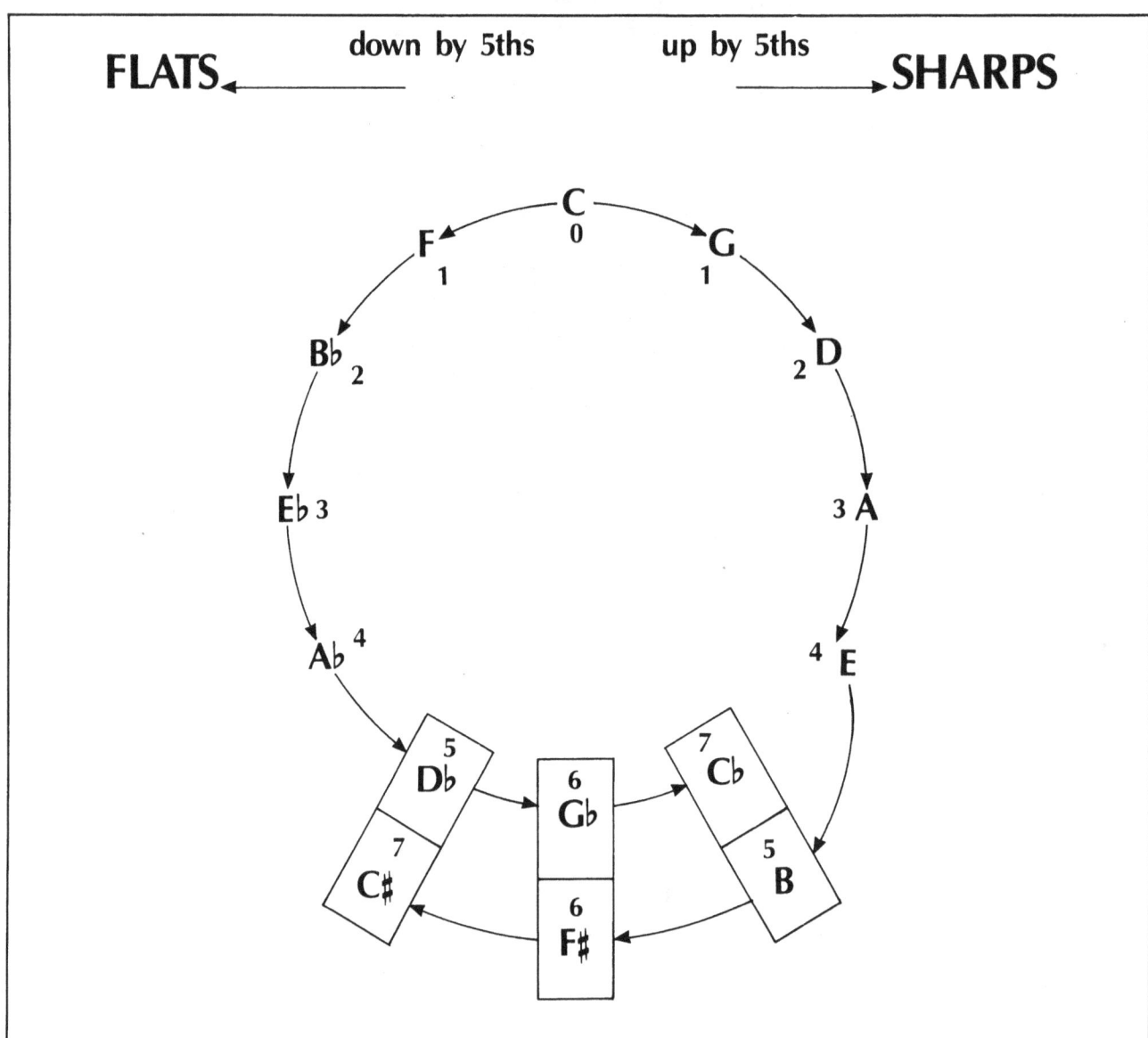

The three pairs of keys in the boxes at the lower end of the circle are known as ENHARMONIC KEYS. They have the same sound but are written differently.

LESSON FOURTEEN

NOTE-NAMING IN SOPRANO, MEZZO-SOPRANO AND BARITONE CLEFS

In Book 1, I briefly mentioned the other positions for the C Clef. The process of note-naming for **C Clef** in any position is as easy as for Treble and Bass Clefs provided that you work in **intervals** as was done in Book 1.

SOPRANO CLEF

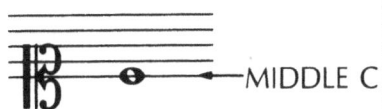 ← MIDDLE C

When the C Clef is placed on the **lowest** line of the staff it is known as the Soprano Clef.

It is seen in early Vocal music up to the time of Brahms (mid 1800s) and is used for the Soprano voice which sings notes from Middle C up, as a general rule.

MEZZO SOPRANO CLEF

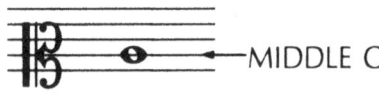 ← MIDDLE C

When the C Clef is placed on the **second** line of the staff it is known as the Mezzo Soprano Clef.

This Clef was in common use before 1750. By placing Middle C on the second line, the notes in the range of the Mezzo-Soprano voice down to the G below Middle C, did not have to be written on Leger Lines.

BARITONE CLEF

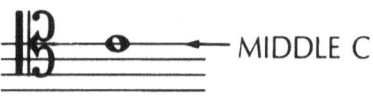 ← MIDDLE C

When the C Clef is placed on the **fifth** line of the staff, it is known as the Baritone Clef.

As the Baritone voice mainly uses notes from Middle C down, this clef adequately covers the range without having to use Leger Lines.

In the following exercises, each Clef should be regarded as your 'front door key' to the puzzle. The Clef shows where Middle C is, and from there you can work out each note by INTERVALS.

Here is the alphabetical list of note-names for you to use when doing the exercises.

A B C D E F G A B C D E F G

◆◆◆◆◆◆◆◆◆◆◆◆◆◆◆◆◆◆◆◆◆◆◆◆◆◆◆◆◆◆◆

EXERCISES

(1) (a) Indicate the intervals between each note in the brackets above the staff.
 (b) Name the notes in the space provided underneath.

SOPRANO CLEF

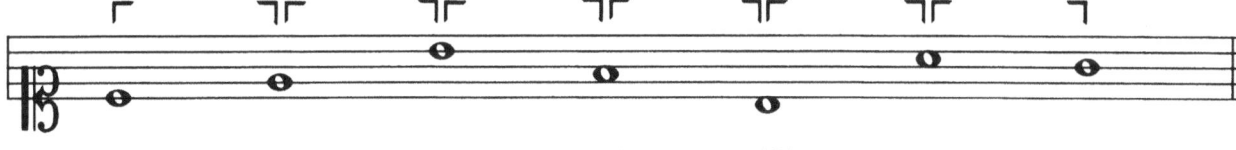

(2) (a) Indicate the intervals between the brackets above the staff.
 (b) Write the required notes on the staff.

MEZZO-SOPRANO CLEF

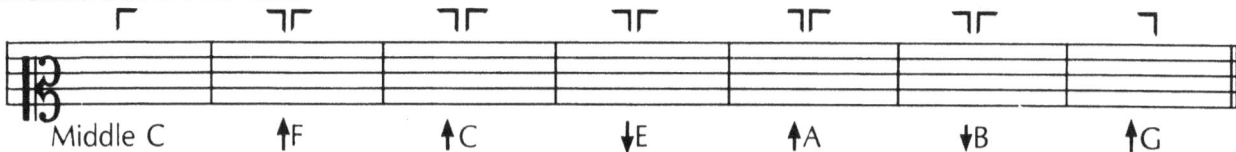

(3) Work out the note names in Baritone Clef using the interval System as before.

LESSON FIFTEEN

MUSICAL TERMS INDICATING TEMPO OR PACE

Several words from the international musical language, Italian, are commonly used to indicate the **speed** at which music should be played.

Another group of words is used to indicate **change of pace**, that is faster or slower.

TEMPO MARKINGS		CHANGE OF PACE	
ITALIAN WORD	**ENGLISH MEANING**	**ITALIAN WORD**	**ENGLISH MEANING**
slow { GRAVE	—slow and solemn	Accelerando (Accel.)	—gradually becoming faster
LARGO	—slow and broad		
LENTO	—slowly	Ritardando (Rit.)	—gradually becoming slower
ADAGIO	—at ease - leisurely	Rallentando (Rall.)	
moderate { ANDANTE	—at an easy walking pace	Ritenuto (Riten.)	—immediately slower - held back
MODERATO	—at a moderate pace	A Tempo	—return to the original speed
ALLEGRETTO	—rather quickly but not as lively as Allegro	Mosso	—movement or speed
		Meno	—less
fast { ALLEGRO	—quickly	Più	—more
VIVACE	—lively and fast	Meno Mosso	—less speed (slower)
PRESTO	—very fast	Più Mosso	—more speed (faster)
PRESTISSIMO	—extremely fast		

◆◆◆◆◆◆◆◆◆◆◆◆◆◆◆◆◆◆◆◆◆◆◆◆◆◆◆

EXERCISE

COMPLETE THESE SENTENCES

1. The slowest Tempo Marking is ....

2. Vivace means ....

3. The two words meaning gradually becoming slower are .... and ....

4. .... means play extremely fast.

5. 'A Tempo' means ....

6. The Italian word which means play at an easy walking pace is ....

7. .... means rather quickly but not as lively as Allegro.

8. The Italian word which means gradually becoming faster is .... which is similar to the English word 'Accelerate'.

LESSON SIXTEEN

SIXTEENTH NOTES OR SEMIQUAVERS

In Part A we learnt about Note and Rest shapes and their values. The next value is the **Sixteenth Note** or **Semiquaver**. It is known as a Sixteenth Note because 16 of them take up the same time span as a Whole Note. The name Semiquaver indicates that the note is half the value of the Quaver. (Semi means half).

Here is the Chart of the Notes and Rests once more with the Sixteenth Note/Semiquaver added.

Note-Shape	American Name	British Name	Duration	Rest-Shape
o	Whole Note	Semibreve	4 counts	
	Half Note	Minim	2 counts	
	Quarter Note	Crotchet	1 count	
	Eighth Note	Quaver	½ of 1 count	
	Sixteenth Note	Semiquaver	¼ of 1 count	

— Sixteenth Notes can be written singly ( ) or beamed together in groups of two, three or four as needed.

— The Sixteenth Rest has two hooks to match the two tails of the sixteenth note.

— Sixteenth Notes can also be beamed together with eighth notes or quavers, to show the time value of a one count note.

— Rests can be combined with the beamed notes so that the eye can clearly see the grouping into the time value of a one count note.

— To **count** semiquavers when the time-signature uses the 1/4 note as the Beat Note (4/4, 3/4, 2/4) say the **number** plus the unit 'a + a'. *(Pronounced uh and uh)* or the number plus the unit 'e + a'. *(Pronounced ee and uh)*.

For example   4/4 1 a + a 2 a + a 3 a + a 4 a + a   OR   4/4 1 e + a 2 e + a 3 e + a 4 e + a

---

Here are the note values from the largest to the smallest in 4/4 time. The counting for Sixteenth Notes is placed under the boxes which represent the time values. The final bar shows some combined note values and how to count them. Colour code the boxes.

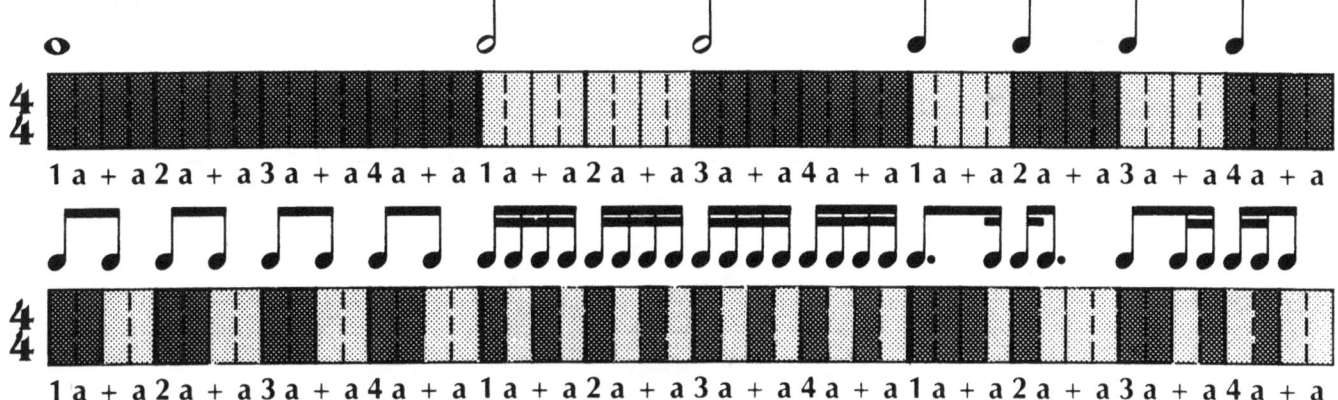

57

LESSON SEVENTEEN

EXERCISES ON SIXTEENTH NOTES

(1) Write the Counting under these bars.

(2) Add the Bar Lines and write the counting under these bars.

(3) First write the counting under the bars then fill in the missing **notes** to complete the bars. Make sure that each beat is completed in turn and that the notes agree with the counts.
Remember not to cross the middle of the bar in 4/4 time.

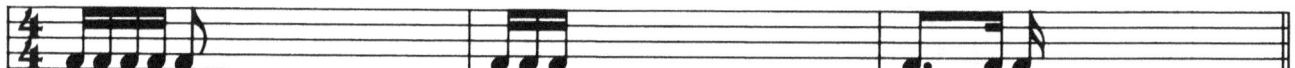

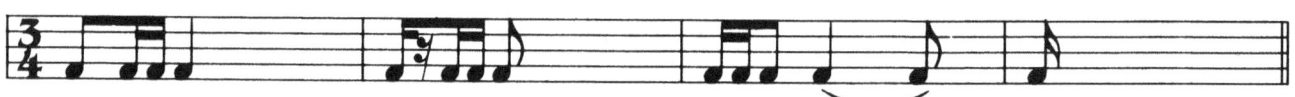

(4) After writing in the counting, fill the missing spaces with **rests**. Complete each beat in turn and group notes and rests to agree with the counts.

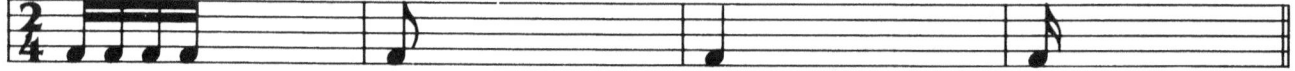

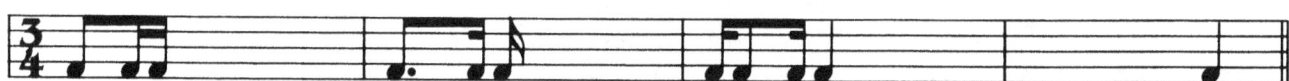

LESSON EIGHTEEN

CHROMATIC SCALE

Apart from the Major Scale which we have already studied, there are several other types of scales which can be used as a basis for composing music. The **Chromatic Scale** is one of these.

The word Chromatic comes from the Greek word 'Chroma' meaning colour. Music that uses the extra notes available in the Chromatic scale is more interesting or 'colourful' to the ear.

The pattern for any Chromatic scale is very simple as it uses only Semitones between each note. As there are twelve semitones in an octave, any Chromatic scale over the range of an Octave will have to play these twelve semitones. When you count the number of notes played and include the Tonic and Upper Tonic notes of the scale, there are in fact THIRTEEN notes to be played.

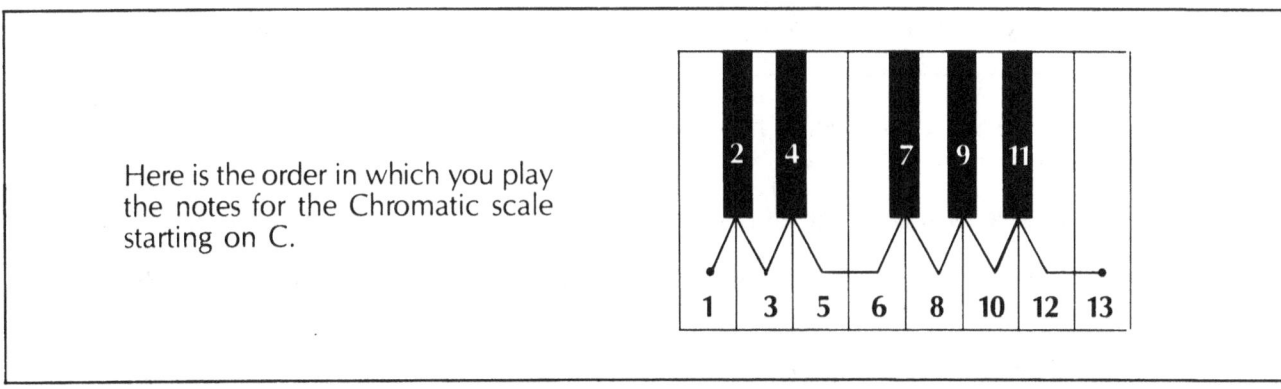

Here is the order in which you play the notes for the Chromatic scale starting on C.

The general rule for writing Chromatic scales is to use SHARPS going UP and FLATS going DOWN. Each Chromatic Scale therefore can be written in the same way provided the starting and finishing notes have been selected.

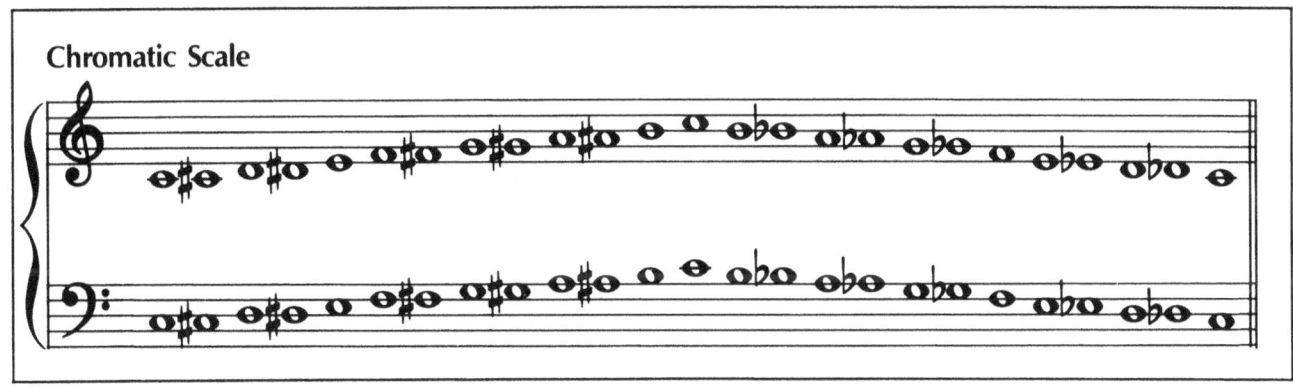

EXERCISES

(1) Write one octave of the Chromatic Scale starting on F ascending only, in the Treble Clef.

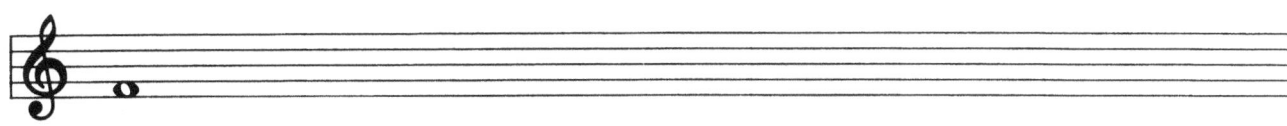

(2) Write one octave of the Chromatic scale starting on A descending only, in the Bass Clef.

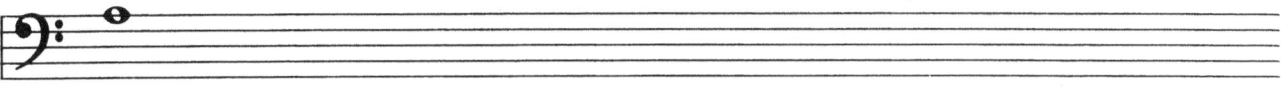

LESSON NINETEEN

MORE SIMPLE METER TIME-SIGNATURES

In Part A you studied three of the Simple Meter Time-Signatures which used the **Quarter Note** or **Crotchet** as the **Beat Note**. They were 2/4, 3/4 and 4/4 time.

Other groups of Time Signatures can occur in Simple Time. One group uses the Half Note or Minim as the Beat Note (A) and the other group uses the Eighth Note or Quaver as the Beat Note (B).

GROUP A 2/2 3/2 4/2	GROUP B 2/8 3/8 4/8
Used more frequently in music before 1750	Used more frequently in music after 1900

Any of the above Time Signatures which have **two** beats in each bar (upper number is 2) are known as **Simple Duple** Time Signatures.

Any which have **three** beats in each bar (upper number is 3) are known as **Simple Triple** Time Signatures.

Any which have **four** beats in each bar (upper number is 4) are known as **Simple Quadruple** Time Signatures.

Here is a chart of all the time signatures studied up to this point, showing the Beat Notes and the Pulses. Remember that the definition of Simple Time is rhythm which uses UNDOTTED notes as Beat Notes. Each **undotted** Beat Note subdivides into TWO pulses.

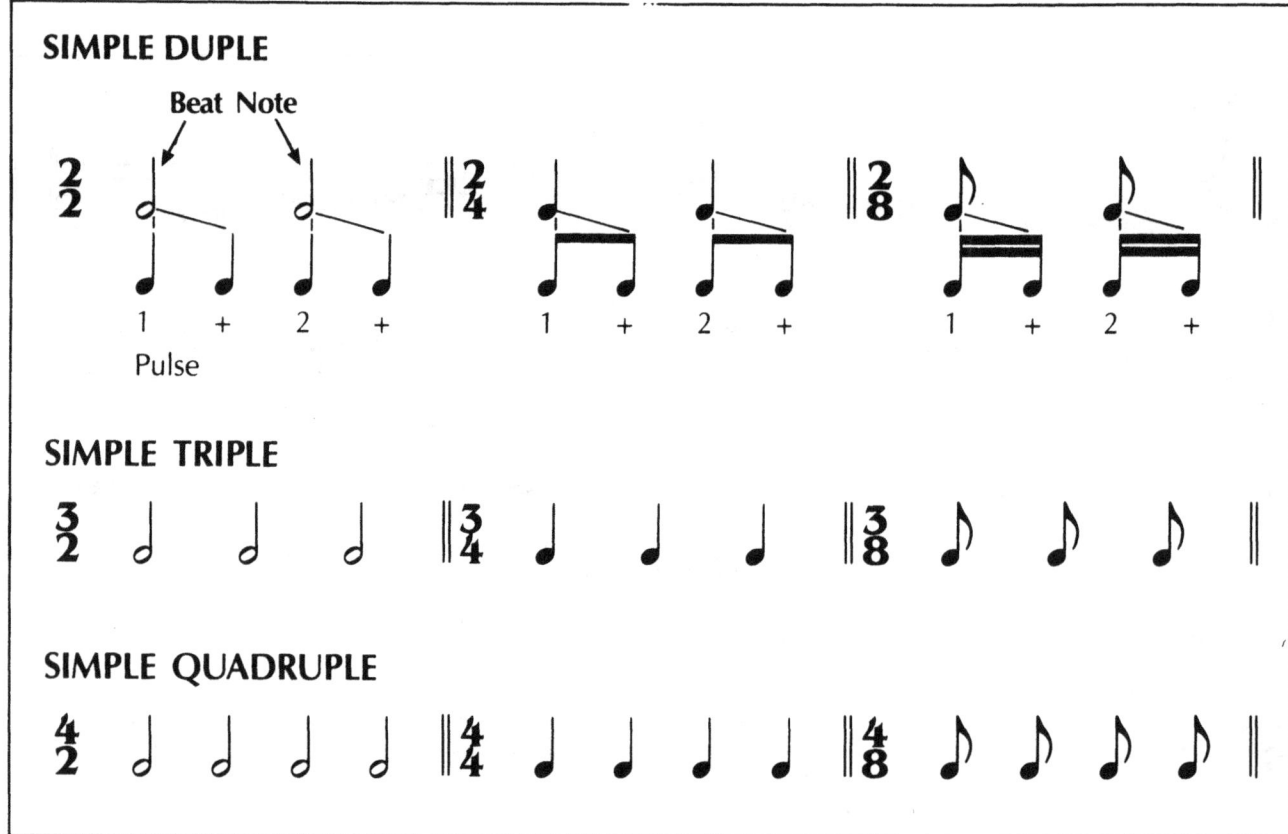

If you read the chart along the line you can see all the time signatures with the same **NUMBER** of Beat Notes. If you read the chart from top to bottom you can see all the time signatures which use the same **TYPE** of Beat Note.

For lessons 19-21 colour highlight the lower number of each time signature and colour any timing diagrams using the standard colours given in the introduction.

LESSON TWENTY

GROUP A TIME-SIGNATURES 2/2 3/2 4/2

As mentioned earlier, these Time-Signatures occur more frequently in early music (before 1750). An older type of note was in use at that time. This note was the BREVE (|o|) which was twice the length of a Semibreve. In the American system it is known as a Double Whole Note. It therefore receives either 8 crotchet counts or 4 minim counts, and can be used to fill a whole bar in 4/2 time.

The three Simple Meter Time-Signatures which use the **Half-Note** or **Minim** as the **Beat Note** are: 2/2, 3/2 and 4/2 time.

Here are the note values that commonly occur in these Time-Signatures. The boxes underneath represent the number of counts each note receives.

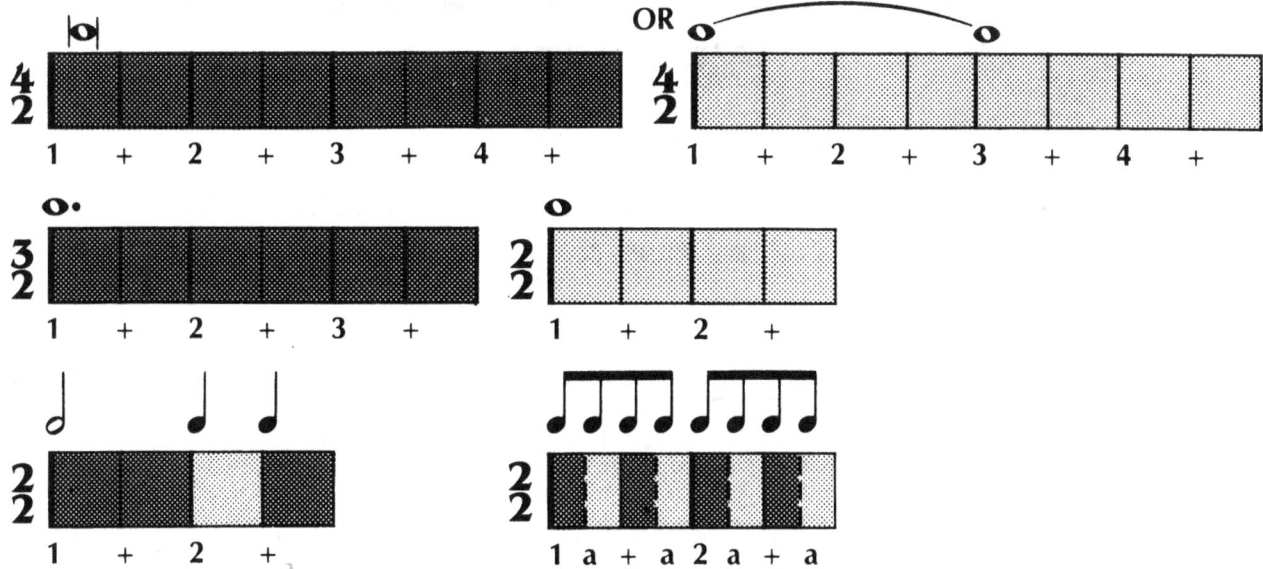

Some examples of music in these Time Signatures are given below.

The examples in 4/2 and 2/2 time follow the rules for 4/4 with each bar being divided into two halves when the notes are grouped together.

The example in 3/2 follows the rules for any Triple time regarding **rests**. A combined rest can be used for beats 1 and 2, while separate rests must be used for beats 2 and 3.

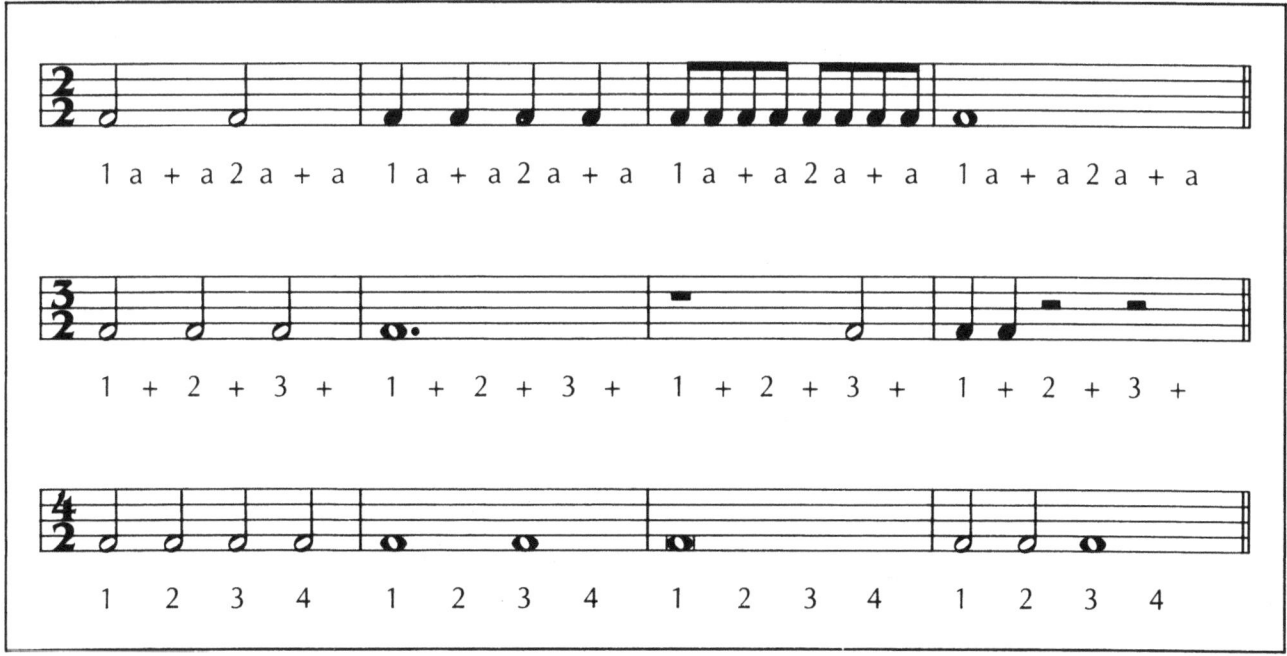

61

LESSON TWENTY-ONE

MORE ON GROUP A TIME SIGNATURES

CUT COMMON TIME ₵

The 2/2 time signature is also known as **Cut Common Time** (Cut Time) or in the British system as **Alla Breve** time. The sign **C** with a cross through it can be written instead of the numbers 2/2.

Music that is written with the Cut Common sign is generally played twice as fast as music in 4/4 time and felt as a DUPLE time signature.

◆◆◆◆◆◆◆◆◆◆◆◆◆◆◆◆◆◆◆◆◆◆◆◆◆◆◆

EXERCISES

(1) Write the counts under these bars.

1 + 2 +   etc.

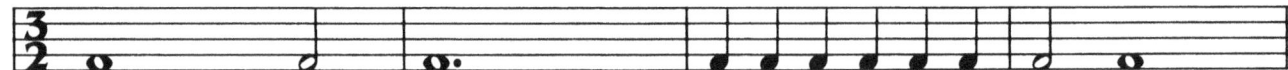

1 a + a   etc.

(2) Add Bar Lines and write the counting under the notes and rests.

(3) Fill in the missing spaces with notes and rests.
Remember the rules for rests in any Triple Time. Combined rests can be used for beats 1 and 2 but separate rests must be used for beats 2 and 3.

LESSON TWENTY-TWO

GROUP B TIME-SIGNATURES 2/8 3/8 4/8

As mentioned in Lesson Nineteen, the three simple Meter Time-Signatures which use the **Eighth Note** or **Quaver** as the **Beat Note** are: 2/8, 3/8 and 4/8 time.

Here are the note values that commonly occur in time-signatures with the Eighth Note as Beat Note. The boxes underneath represent the number of counts each note receives.

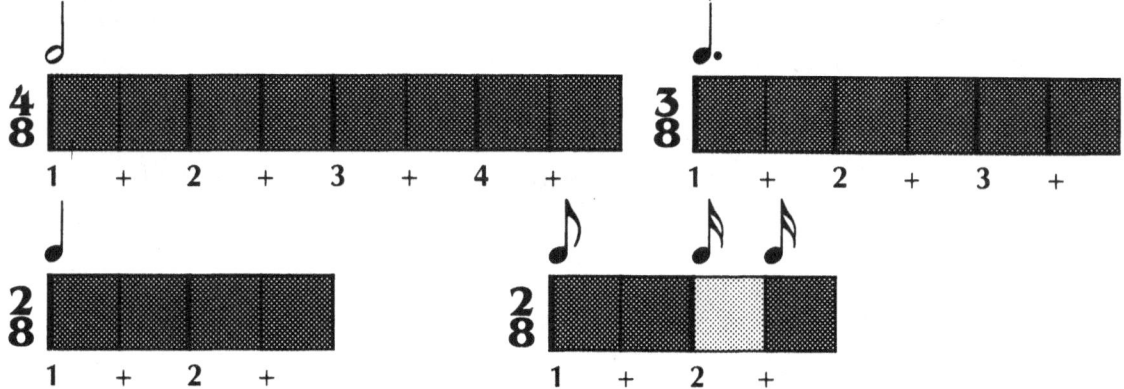

Two Examples of music in 4/8 and 3/8 time are given below. Notice that the example in 4/8 follows the rules for 4/4 with each bar being divided into two halves when the notes are grouped together.

The 3/8 example follows the rules for any Triple time regarding **rests**. The combined rest can be used for beats 1 and 2 while separate rests must be used for beats 2 and 3.

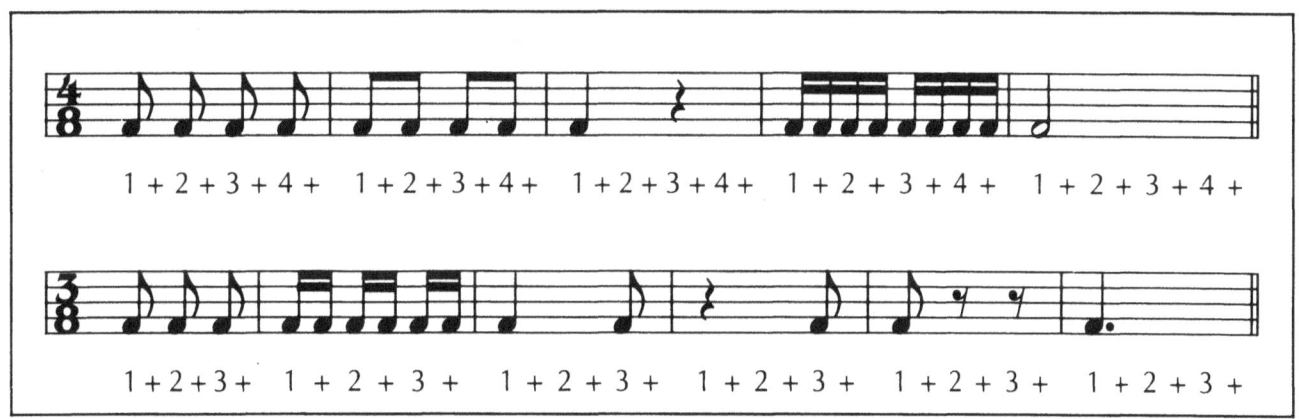

EXERCISE

(1) Write the counts under these bars. Use 'ANDS' for each bar e.g. 1+2+

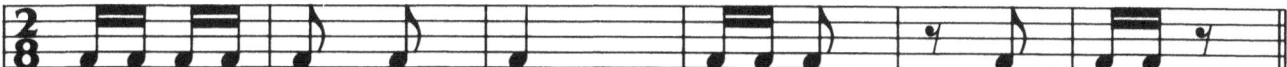

(2) Write the counting under these notes and add the bar lines.

(3) Write the counts below these bars then fill in the missing spaces with notes and rests.

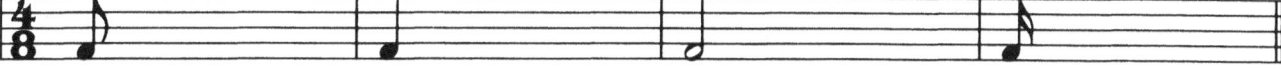

LESSON TWENTY-THREE

TIES AND SLURS

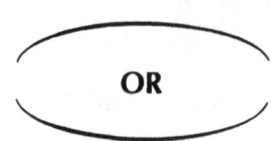

A curved line is often used either between two notes of the same pitch, or covering two or more notes of different pitch.

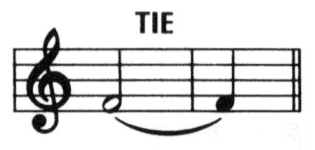

TIE — When the line connects two notes of the same pitch, it is called a Tie. It has the effect of combining the note values of both notes.

1 2 1 2 sounds the same as 1 2 3 4

A Tie is necessary if you need a sound to continue over the bar line, or across the middle of the bar in any Simple Quadruple Time-Signature.

SLUR — When the line covers notes of different pitch it is called a Slur. A Slur indicates that the notes within it are to be played very smoothly.

EXERCISES

(1) Indicate whether the following are ties or slurs.

a .... b ....

c .... d ....

(2) Write the required notes in the boxes then add their values to give the combined count of the tied notes.

(a)  = ... (b)  = ...
    Minim   Crotchet   Dotted Crotchet Quaver

(c)  = ... (d) 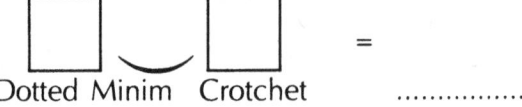 = ...
    Semibreve Minim   Dotted Minim Crotchet

(e)  = ... (f) 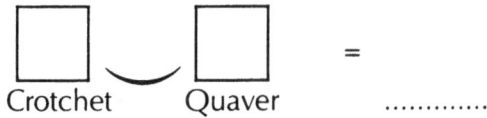 = ...
    Semiquaver Dotted Quaver   Crotchet   Quaver

LESSON TWENTY-FOUR

MORE MUSICAL TERMS, SIGNS AND SYMBOLS

There are several Music Signs which tell you HOW to play the notes.

SLUR  We have already seen the Slur which indicates that the notes should be played smoothly.

Special Note In piano music it is understood that when no markings occur at all, the style in which the music should be played is LEGATO or smoothly.

STACCATO The opposite of the Legato Slur marking is the STACCATO dot. The dot is placed near the head of the note, either above it if the stem goes down, or below the note head if the stem goes up.
The general interpretation of a Staccato dot is to play the note **Detached**. The strict interpretation is that the Staccato dot shortens the note by half its value. However most people as a general rule play the note 'short and crisp.'

ACCENT This sign means play the note with added emphasis, that is louder.

FERMATA This is a PAUSE sign. It means hold the note for longer than written value. It is often used at the end of a piece so that the performer can linger on the last note.
e.g. a four count note (𝅝) with a FERMATA sign could be held for six counts if the performer so desired.

⌐ ¬
|8va   This sign is short for the Italian word OTTAVA. If it is placed **above** a group of notes
- - -   it means play them an octave **higher**. If it is placed **below** a group of notes it means
        play them an octave **lower**. Sometimes the word 'Basso' is also placed next to it to confirm
or   that the notes should be played lower. i.e. 8va Basso.
- - -
|8va
⌐ ¬

LOCO This is the Italian word for 'in place'. It is used after an 8va sign to indicate that the music should be played in the written position.

◆◆◆◆◆◆◆◆◆◆◆◆◆◆◆◆◆◆◆◆◆◆◆◆◆◆◆◆

EXERCISE

Complete these sentences.

1. A note with an Accent (𝆓) above it has to be played ....

2. A note with a Pause sign (𝄐) FERMATA above it is to be ....

3. 8va placed above a group of notes means that they have to be played ....

4. The Slur indicates that the notes should be played ....

5. A note with a Staccato dot above it (𝅘𝅥) is played ....

6. A Tie connects two notes of the .... pitch.

7. The word that means play in the written position, and is used after 8va is ....

LESSON TWENTY-FIVE

MAJOR AND MINOR THIRDS

Apart from what we already know as the interval of a THIRD between two notes (written Line to Line or Space to Space) there are also **larger** and **smaller** sounding versions of the third.

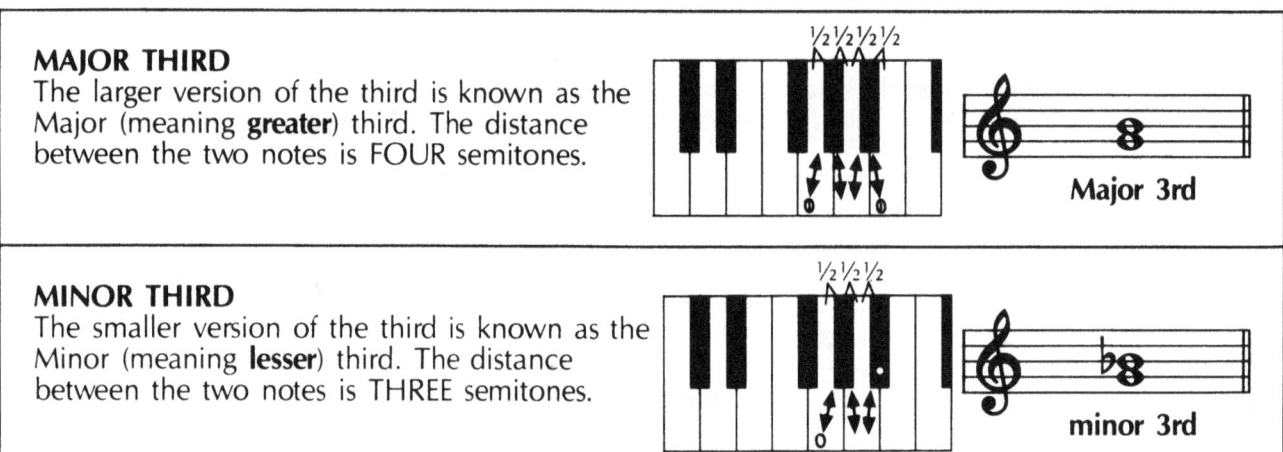

MAJOR THIRD
The larger version of the third is known as the Major (meaning **greater**) third. The distance between the two notes is FOUR semitones.

MINOR THIRD
The smaller version of the third is known as the Minor (meaning **lesser**) third. The distance between the two notes is THREE semitones.

The Major and Minor thirds are the fundamental building blocks of many chords.

COUNTING SEMITONES
When counting semitones, it is wise to go to a keyboard and depress two keys at a time.

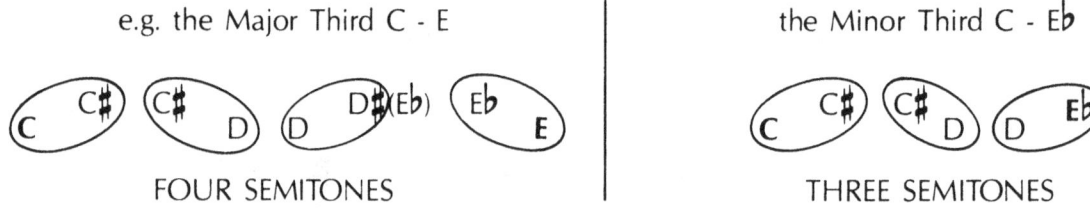

e.g. the Major Third C - E — FOUR SEMITONES

the Minor Third C - E♭ — THREE SEMITONES

Accidental Chart

This chart presents the Accidentals in progressive order from **Lowest** to **Highest**, with a semitone between each one. Keep this chart in mind when raising or lowering notes by a semitone.

e.g. — The note a semitone higher than G♭♭ is G♭
— The note a semitone lower than F♯ is F♮.

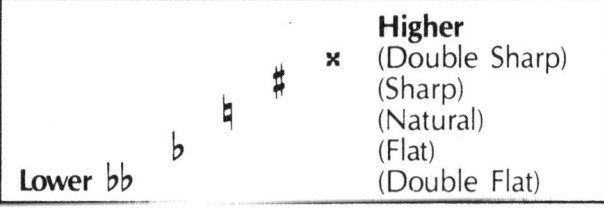

Higher
× (Double Sharp)
♯ (Sharp)
♮ (Natural)
♭ (Flat)
Lower ♭♭ (Double Flat)

◆◆◆◆◆◆◆◆◆◆◆◆◆◆◆◆◆◆◆◆◆◆◆◆◆◆◆◆

EXERCISE

(1) Indicate whether the following are Major or Minor thirds. (Maj3/mi3)

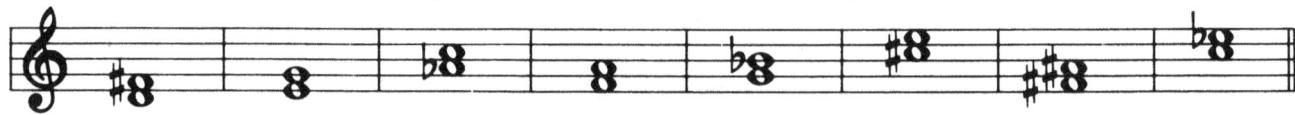

(2) First draw thirds above each note, then alter the accidentals if needed to form Major Thirds (Maj3) or Minor Thirds (mi3) as required.

Maj3   mi3   Maj3   Maj3   mi3   Maj3   mi3   mi3

LESSON TWENTY-SIX

THE MAJOR TRIAD

A **CHORD** is a combination of three or more notes.
A **TRIAD** is a three-note chord.
A **Major Triad** can be approached from many points of view. Two of them are presented here. Further approaches can be found in my Contemporary Chord Workbook, Book 1.

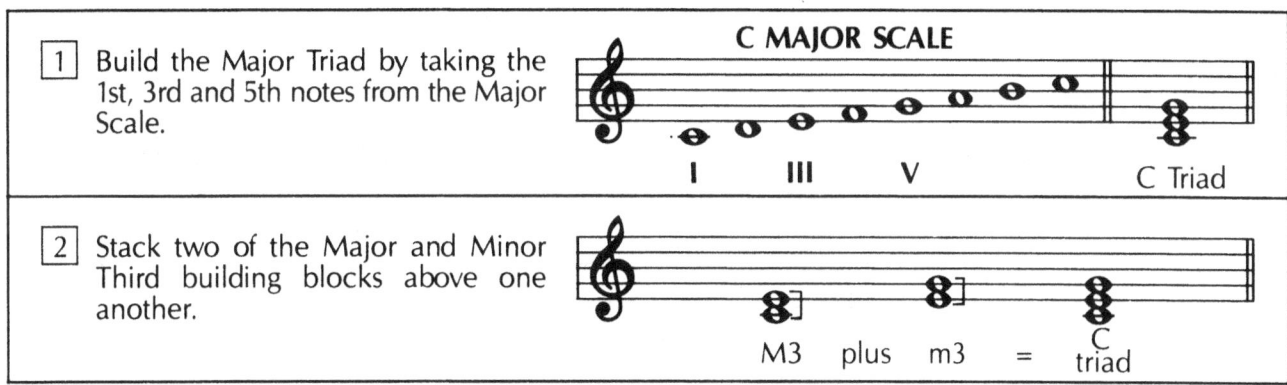

Colour Code	FORMULA FOR A MAJOR TRIAD 3/4
• red for 3	mi3 = 3 semitones
• blue for 4	Maj3 = 4 semitones

Note the larger number at the base of the triad.

CHORD SYMBOL — The convention in Modern Chord naming is to identify a Major Triad by its letter name only. e.g. D = D Major Triad.

◆◆◆◆◆◆◆◆◆◆◆◆◆◆◆◆◆◆◆◆◆◆◆◆◆◆◆◆

EXERCISES

(1) Write the Major Scales beginning on the given notes, then extract the First, Third and Fifth notes to form the Major Triad.

[I] II [III] IV [V] VI VII VIII   Chord

(2) Alter the accidentals if needed to convert these chords to Major Triads.

(3) Build Major Triads above the given notes using Approach Number 2.

Maj3 + mi3 = Major Triad

e.g. 4 semitones Plus 3 semitones = D   +   = ...
         (+)

    +   = ...   +   = ...

LESSON TWENTY-SEVEN

THE MINOR TRIAD

Here are two ways of approaching the **Minor Triad.**

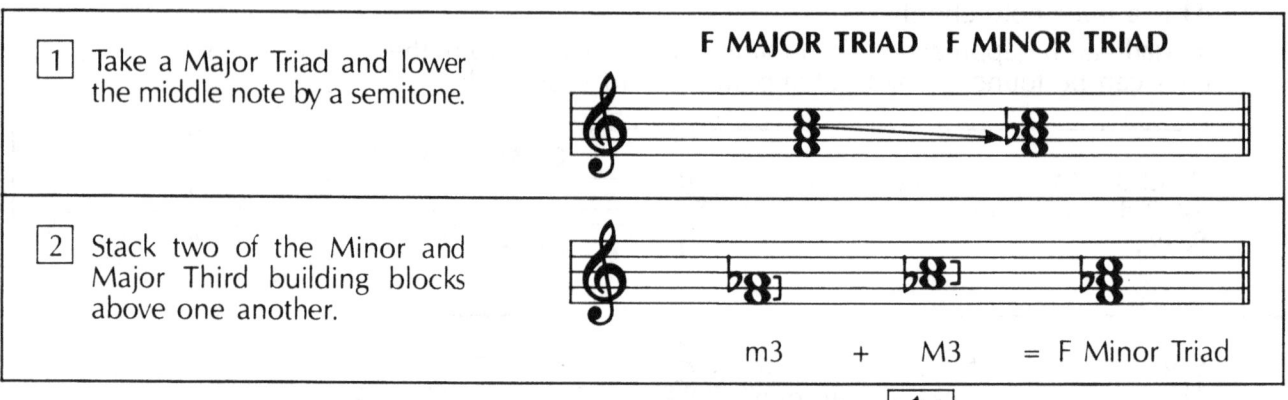

FORMULA FOR A MINOR TRIAD

Maj3 = 4 semitones ‖ *Note the smaller number at the base of the triad.*
mi3 = 3 semitones

(N.B. A MINOR TRIAD can also be formed by combining the 1st, 3rd and 5th degrees (notes) from a Minor scale. Refer to Book 2 in this series.)

CHORD SYMBOL — The convention in Modern Chord naming is to identify a Minor Triad by its letter name followed by a lower case 'm' or 'mi'.

◆◆◆◆◆◆◆◆◆◆◆◆◆◆◆◆◆◆◆◆◆◆◆◆◆

EXERCISES

(1) Rewrite the Major Chords from Question One on the previous page, then lower the middle note of each to form Minor Triads.

(2) Build Minor Triads above the given notes using Approach Number 2.

(3) First build triad shapes above each given note, then alter the accidentals if needed to convert the chords to Minor Triads.

Triad Shape | Accidental Added

(4) Name these chords as either Major or Minor.

LESSON TWENTY-EIGHT

THE DIMINISHED TRIAD

The word **Diminish** means to **make smaller**.

A **Diminished Triad** is constructed of two of the smaller thirds (minor thirds; 3 semitones) which makes the chord smaller than the Major and Minor triads.

Two of the ways to approach a Diminished Triad are:

[1] Take a Major Triad and **lower** both the Third and Fifth degrees by a semitone.

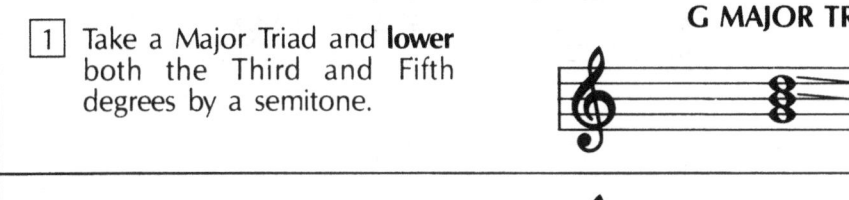

[2] Stack two of the Minor Third building blocks above one another.

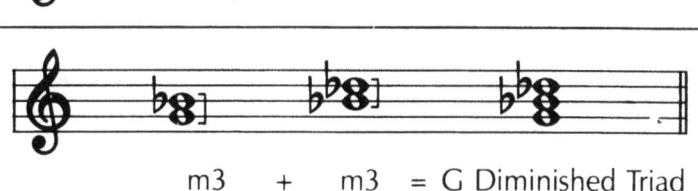

m3 + m3 = G Diminished Triad

FORMULA FOR A DIMINISHED TRIAD $\begin{array}{c}3\\3\end{array}$

mi3 = 3 semitones
mi3 = 3 semitones

CHORD SYMBOL — The convention in Modern Chord naming is to use a **small circle** following the letter name to indicate a Diminished Triad. e.g. D° = D Diminished Triad. In some publications the word 'dim' is also used.

◆◆◆◆◆◆◆◆◆◆◆◆◆◆◆◆◆◆◆◆◆◆◆◆◆◆◆◆◆

EXERCISES

(1) First write the Major Triad above the given note, then lower the Third and Fifth degrees to build Diminished Triads on the same note.

e.g. A   A°

(2) Build Diminished Triads above the given notes using Approach Number 2.

mi3 + mi3 = dim Triad

e.g. semitones + semitones = E°   +   = ...

+   = ...   +   = ...

(3) Write Major, Minor and Diminished chords above each given note.

e.g. F   Fm   F°

Formula: 3   4   3
         4   3   3

LESSON TWENTY-NINE

THE AUGMENTED TRIAD

The word **Augment** means to **make larger**.
An **Augmented Triad** is constructed of two of the larger thirds (Major thirds; 4 semitones) which makes the chord larger than the Major chord.
Two of the ways to approach an Augmented Triad are:

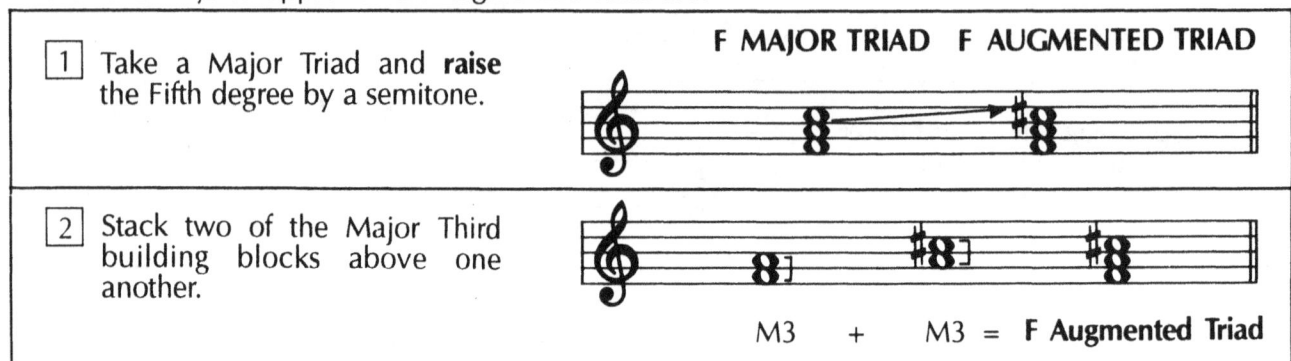

1. Take a Major Triad and **raise** the Fifth degree by a semitone.

2. Stack two of the Major Third building blocks above one another.

FORMULA FOR THE AUGMENTED TRIAD

Maj3 = 4 semitones
Maj3 = 4 semitones

CHORD SYMBOL — The convention in Modern Chord naming is to indicate an Augmented triad by using a **plus sign** after the letter name. e.g. F^+ = F Augmented Triad. In some publications the word 'aug' is also used.

◆◆◆◆◆◆◆◆◆◆◆◆◆◆◆◆◆◆◆◆◆◆◆◆◆◆

EXERCISES

N.B. Flats and Sharps may occur in the same chord.

(1) First write the Major Triad above the given notes then raise the fifth degree by a semitone to build Augmented triads above the same notes.

e.g.   D D^+

(2) Build Augmented Triads above the given notes using Approach Number 2.

e.g.   semitones + semitones = C^+

+ = ...   + = ...

(3) Name these chords as either Diminished or Augmented.

(4) Write Major, Minor, Diminished and Augmented Triads above the given notes.

e.g.   G   Gm G^o G^+
          3   4   3   4
Formula: 4   3   3   4

LESSON THIRTY

THE SUSPENDED FOURTH TRIAD

There is one other triad in common use today, the **Suspended Fourth triad**.
Two of the ways to approach a Suspended Fourth Triad are:

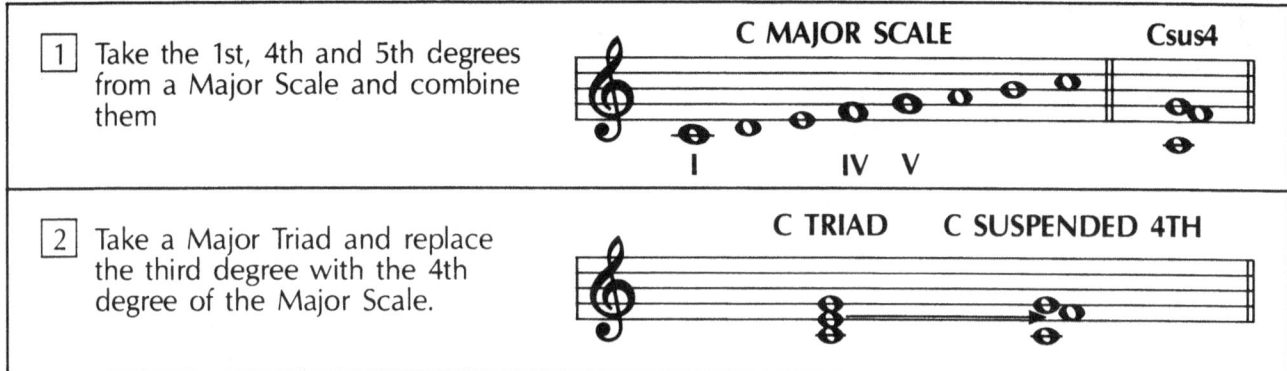

1. Take the 1st, 4th and 5th degrees from a Major Scale and combine them

2. Take a Major Triad and replace the third degree with the 4th degree of the Major Scale.

CHORD SYMBOL — The convention in Modern Chord naming is to identify a Suspended Fourth triad by the short form of the word 'sus4' or simply 'sus', the 4 being understood.

TRIAD REVIEW

Here are the formulae in semitones of the triads covered on the previous pages.

MAJOR	MINOR	DIMINISHED	AUGMENTED
3	4	3	4
4	3	3	4

The Major Triad can be altered to form the above triads, and the Suspended Fourth triad in the following ways:

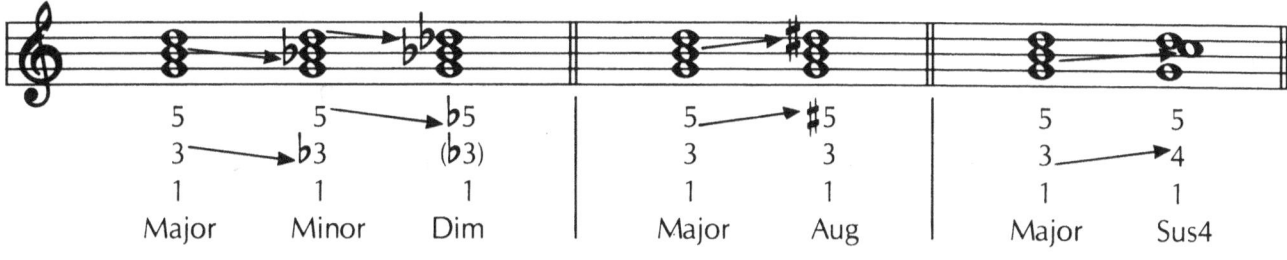

EXERCISES

(1) Write the Major scales of the given notes then extract the 1st, 4th and 5th degrees to build Suspended 4th chords on the same notes.

(2) Write the Major Triads and Suspended Fourth Triads on the given notes using Approach Number 2.

(3) Write the five types of triad above the given notes.

LESSON THIRTY-ONE

MAJOR AND MINOR CHORDS IN INVERSIONS

Root Position

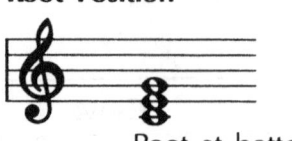
Root at bottom

— The original position of the chord, found when the First, Third and Fifth degrees are taken from the scale, is called the **Root Position**.

— The lowest note in a Root Position chord is known as the **Root Note**, the note from which the chord grows.

Inversions

— To invert means to turn upside down.

— An inversion of a chord is created when the notes have been turned upside down and re-arranged.

— A triad can be inverted twice.

First Inversion

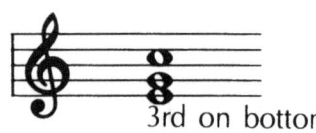
3rd on bottom

— When the lowest note of the Root Position chord is moved up an octave so that it becomes the top note of the chord, the chord is in **First Inversion**.

Second Inversion

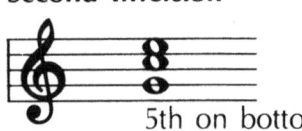
5th on bottom

— When the lowest note of the First Inversion chord is moved up an octave so it becomes the top note of the next chord, the chord is in **Second Inversion**.

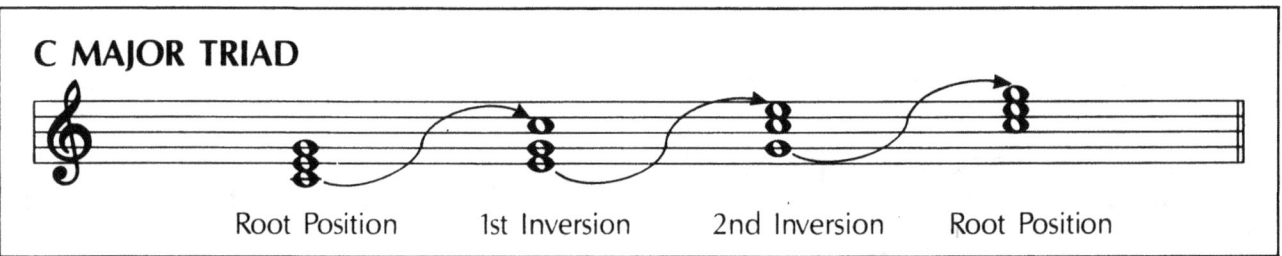

The inversions of Major and Minor Triads can easily be recognised by the intervals between the notes.

The diagram below shows where the intervals occur. The Root Note of the chord in each inversion is also indicated, by the arrows.

When trying to find the name of an inverted chord first bring it back to its ROOT POSITION and then use one of the methods you have learned to find out its quality, i.e. Major or Minor.

To write chords in inversions, either take the lowest note up an octave each time, or follow this procedure:

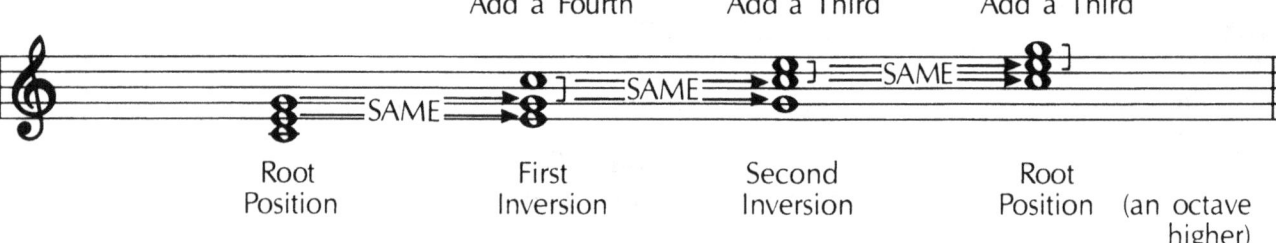

LESSON THIRTY-TWO

EXERCISES ON INVERSIONS

(1) Write the following Major and Minor chords in inversions.
   If an accidental occurs on one of the notes, it must be transferred up the octave together with the note.

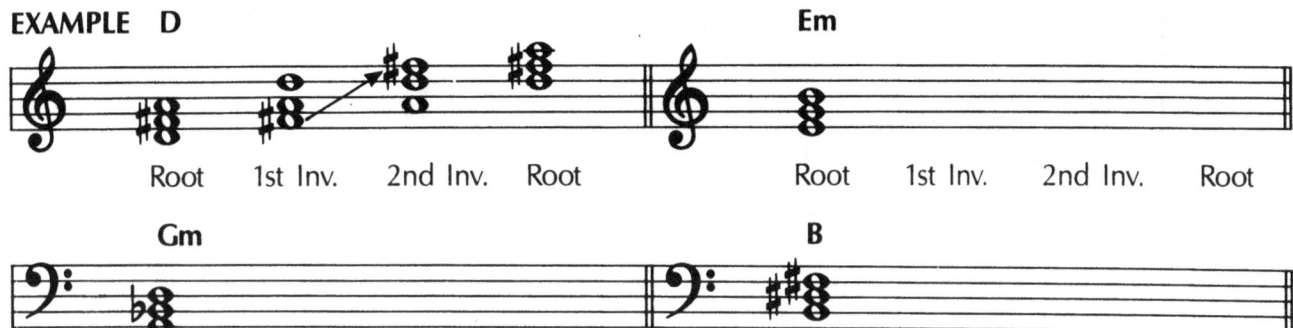

(2) Pick the shapes of these triads by the intervals between the notes. Root Position = Thirds only; First Inversion = fourth at the top; Second Inversion = fourth at the bottom.

Also indicate where the Root Note of the triad is located; i.e. at the **Bottom**, in the **Middle** or on the **Top**.

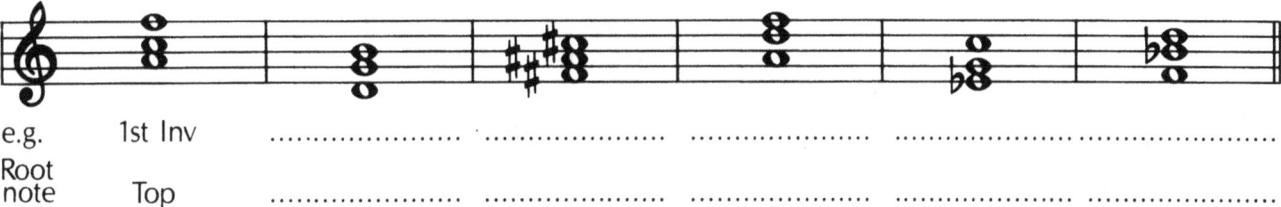

e.g.   1st Inv   ....
Root
note   Top   ....

(3) Rewrite these chords as Root Position chords, then name them. If the chord is in First Inversion, take the top note **down** an octave to find the Root Position.
   If the chord is in Second Inversion, take the bottom note **up** an octave to find the Root Position.

e.g.   B   ....

DIMINISHED AND AUGMENTED CHORDS IN INVERSIONS

To invert a Diminished or Augmented chord follow the same procedure as for Major and Minor chords.

(4) Write the following Diminished and Augmented chords in inversions.

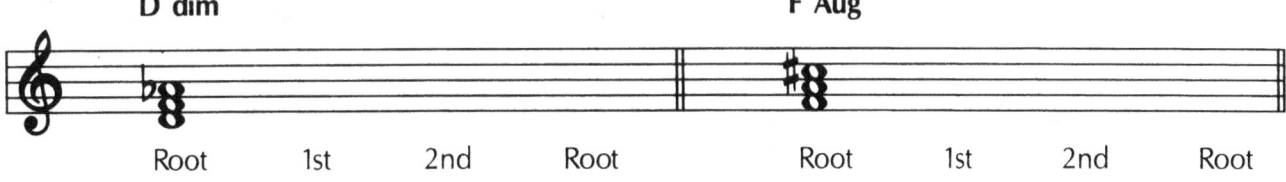

(5) Write the following chords in Root Position and all inversions.

   C dim   **G Aug**

   (bass clef staff)

   Root   1st   2nd   Root   Root   1st   2nd   Root

LESSON THIRTY-THREE

SUSPENDED FOURTH TRIADS IN INVERSIONS

The **Suspended Fourth Triad** looks quite different to the other four types of triad whether in Root Position or in an inversion.

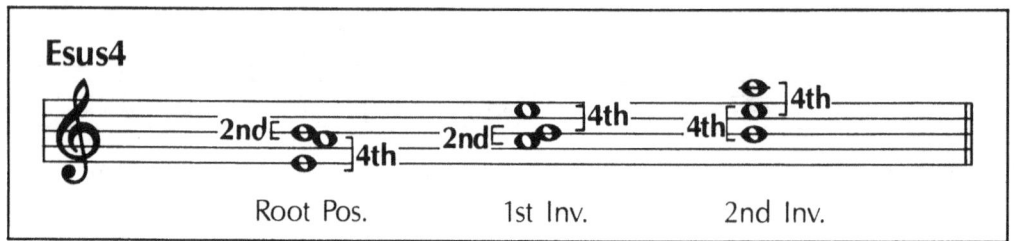

Intervals	2nd on top	4th on top	4th on top
	4th on bottom	2nd on bottom	4th on bottom

The interval of the 4th is the clue to the inversion of the chord.
If it is on the bottom only, the chord is in Root Position.
If it is at the top only, the chord is in First Inversion.
If there are two fourths in the chord, it is in Second Inversion.

◆◆◆◆◆◆◆◆◆◆◆◆◆◆◆◆◆◆◆◆◆◆◆◆◆◆◆

EXERCISES

(1) Write the inversions of these Suspended Fourth triads.

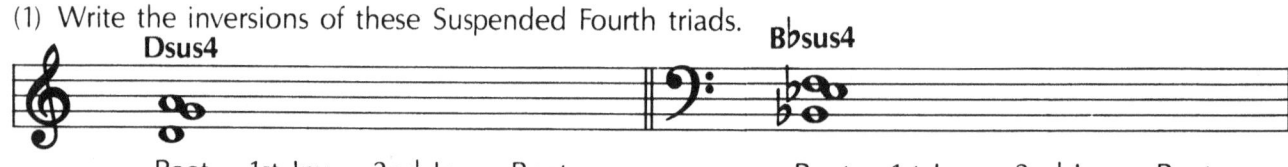

(2) Write the Root Position and all inversions of these Suspended Fourth Triads.

(3) Name these Root Position chords as either Maj, Min, Dim, Aug or Sus.

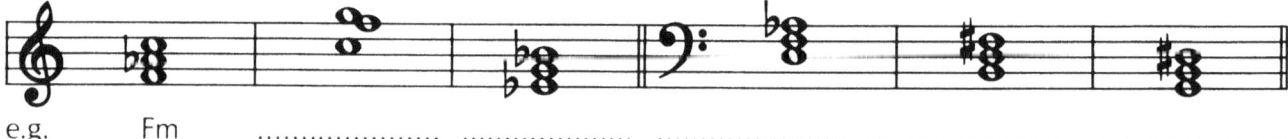

e.g.   Fm

(4) Name these First inversion triads. Remember that the Root Note is on top. Take it down an octave to find the Root Position.

e.g.   E dim

(5) Name these Second Inversion triads. Remember to take the lowest note up an octave to find the Root Position.

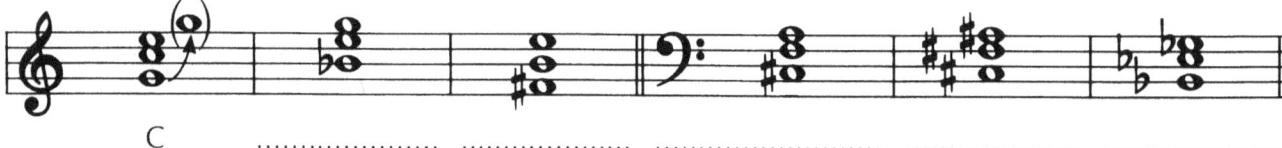

C

LESSON THIRTY-FOUR

REPEAT SIGNS

There are several signs used in music to indicate that the music should be repeated.

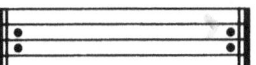

1. **DOUBLE DOTS** When a segment needs to be repeated without change, a pair of dots is placed on the second and third spaces of the staff, next to the double bar lines.

Sometimes when the music is to be repeated from the beginning, there will only be one set of Double Dots at the end of the section.

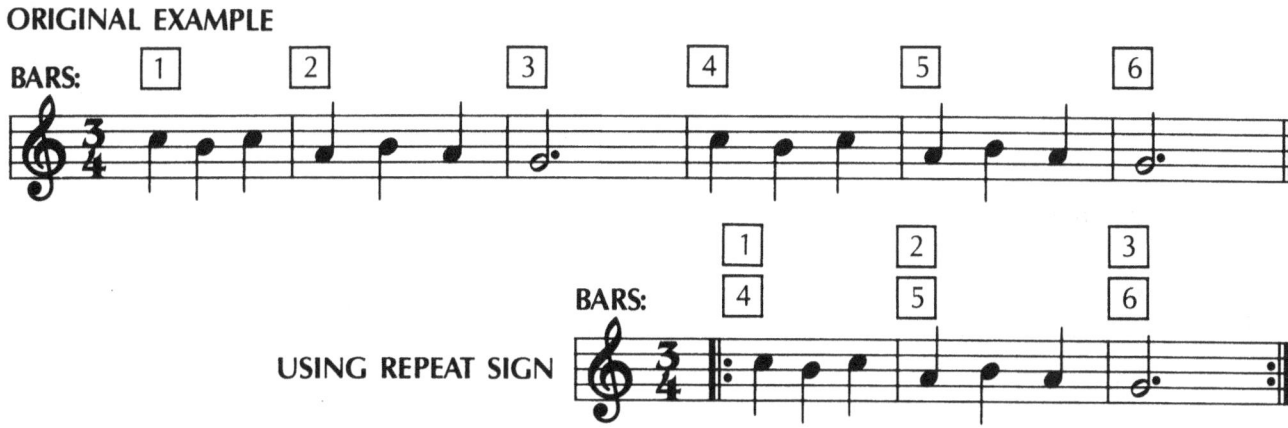

2. **1ST & 2ND ENDINGS** When the majority of the music needs to be repeated exactly, except for the last few bars, 1st and 2nd endings can be used to save space.

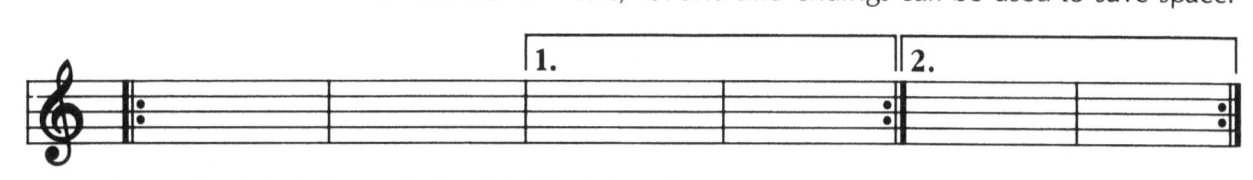

In the example below, bars 1, 2 and 3 are the same as bars 6, 7 and 8. The different bars, Nos 4 and 5, are played the first time, so they can be included in the 1st Ending or First Time Bar. Bars 9 and 10 are only played the second time, so they can be included in the 2nd Ending or Second Time Bar.

The First Ending has a Repeat Sign (Double Dots). The bars under the First ending are only played the first time through. They are skipped over on the repeat playing, and the Second Ending is played.

This can be written with 1st and 2nd endings:

LESSON THIRTY-FIVE

EXERCISES ON REPEAT SIGNS

(1) Rewrite this four bar melody as a two bar melody with a Repeat Sign.

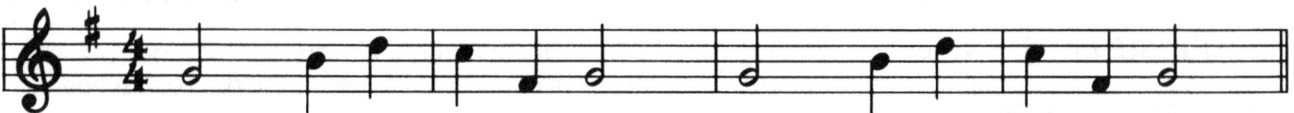

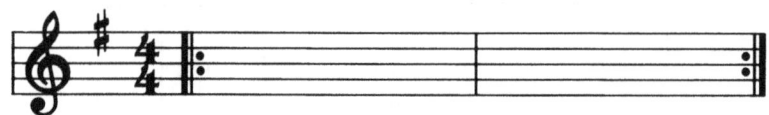

(2) Rewrite this melody using 1st and 2nd Endings.

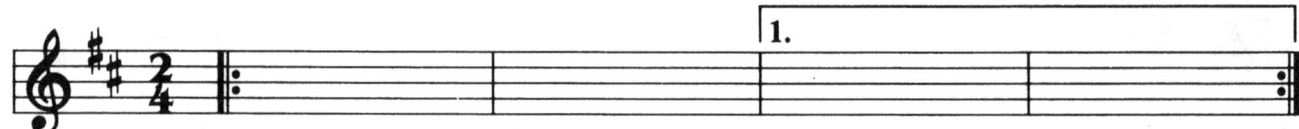

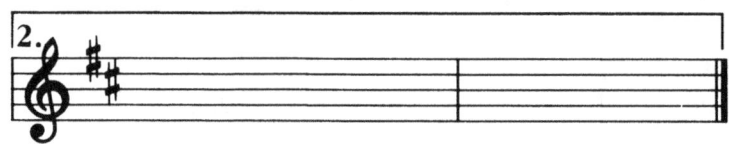

(3) Write this melody out in full without using 1st and 2nd Endings.

LESSON THIRTY-SIX

THIRD ENDINGS

The system of 1st and 2nd Endings can be extended to a 3rd Ending and sometimes even a 4th. Often the words 'Play Three Times' or 'Play Four Times' are written above the first bar, to make the composer's intention very clear.

EXERCISE

Rewrite this melody using 1st, 2nd and 3rd Endings.

PLAY THREE TIMES

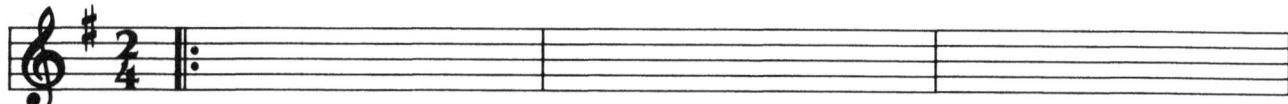

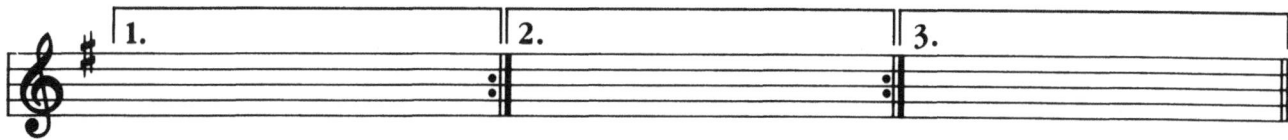

77

LESSON THIRTY-SEVEN

TEST YOUR KNOWLEDGE

Fill in the blanks.

(1) [musical notation] is the interval of a ....

(2) To find the next Flat Key Signature in the Cycle of Fifths you go .... A Fifth from the Upper Tonic of the scale.

(3) A Minor 3rd contains .... semitones.

(4) Very High C and Very Low C are both written .... Leger Lines away from the staff.

(5) The first four flats in the order or flats in a key Signature spell the word ....

(6) A Major Triad can be built by taking the ...., ... and .... degrees from a Major Scale.

(7) The 7 sharps in the order they come in the Key Signature are ....

(8) Presto means to play ....

(9) ....Semiquavers fit into a Whole Note (Semibreve).

(10) All Simple Quadruple Time Signatures have .... as the Top Number.

(11) The .... Triad has the formula in semitones $\frac{3}{3}$.

(12) The intervals in the Line to Line, Space to Space family are the ....

(13) E Major Scale has 4 sharps; the key signature with one sharp more is ....

(14) Fortissimo is the Italian word for ....

(15) Three Simple Triple time signatures are ...., ... and ....

(16) The word Augment means to ....

(17) The degree names for the First and Fifth degrees of the scale are ....and....................

(18) [musical notation] is a .... Clef.

(19) Apart from the Root Position of a Triad there are .... inversions.

(20) The Key signature of E Flat Major has .... flats which are ....

(21) ₵ is the sign for ....

(22) In a Major scale there are .... Tetrachords, which both have the same structure,

........................, ..., ...

(23) [musical notation] is a ....

(24) A dot placed above or below a note means that the note should be played ....

(25) The five types of triad are ...., ..., ..., ... and ....

78

ANSWER SHEET

Lesson One: Q.1 7th, 8ve, 6th, 7th, 6th, 8ve

Q.2

Q.3

Lesson Two: Q.1 A, A, B, A, B, B, B, A
Q.2 Prime, 8ve, 4th, 6th, 2nd, 7th, 5th, 3rd

Q.3

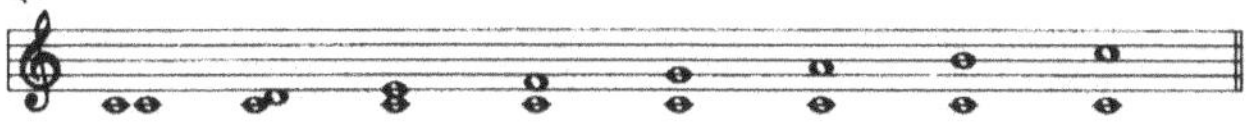

Lesson Three: Q.1a Intervals: 3rd, 6th, 7th, 3rd, 8ve, 7th
Names: A C B G G F
Q.1b Intervals: 7th, 2nd, 8ve, 2nd, 6th, 5th
Names: B C D B E

Q.2 7th, 6th, 8ve, 5th, 7th, 6th
↓D ↑B ↑B (↓) ↑G ↑F ↑A

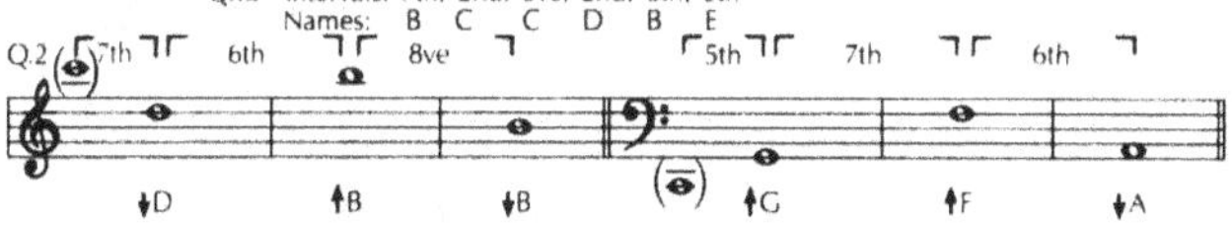

Lesson Four: 1. piano, soft 2. very loud 3. ⟨crescendo⟩ 4. mp 5. gradually softer
6. forte fortissimo, very, very loud 7. very 8. ⟨decrescendo⟩

Lesson Five: 1. Tonic 2. Vth 3. Mediant 4. Subdominant 5. Submediant 6. IInd
7. VIIth, Leading Note

Lesson Six:

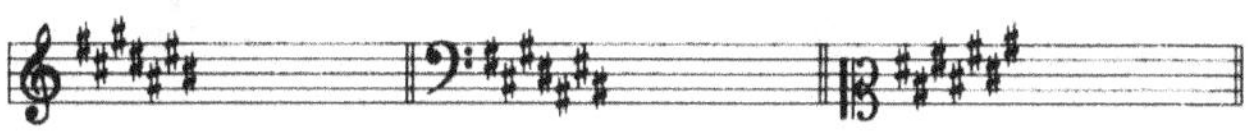

Lesson Seven:
Q.1

Q.2

Lesson Nine: A

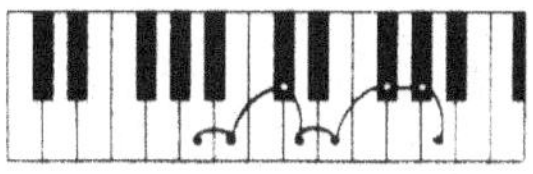

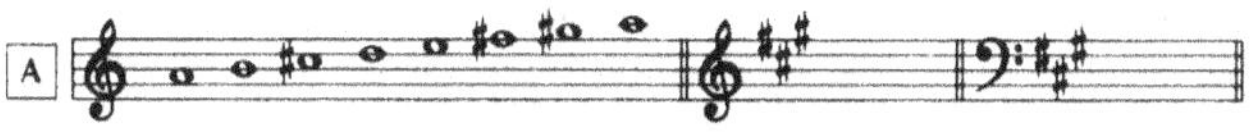

Lesson Ten: E

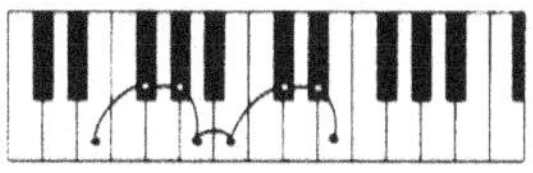

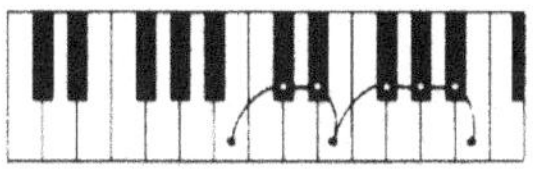

B

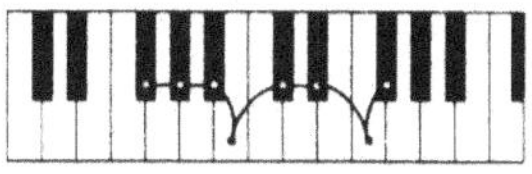

F#

C#

Lesson Eleven Eb

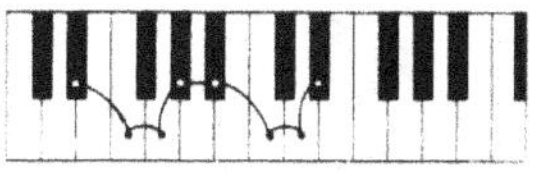

Lesson Twelve: Ab

Db

Gb

Cb

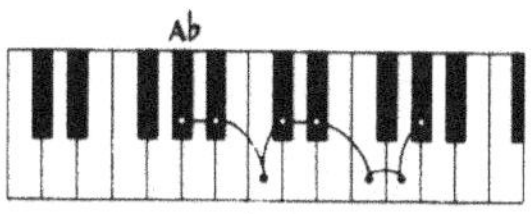

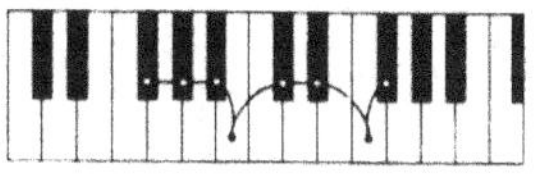

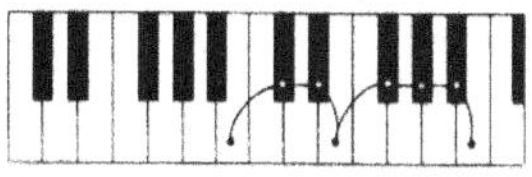

Lesson Fourteen: Q.1 Intervals: 3rd, 5th, 4th, 5th, 7th, 2nd
Names C E B F B A G
Q.2 4th, 5th, 6th, 4th, 7th, 6th

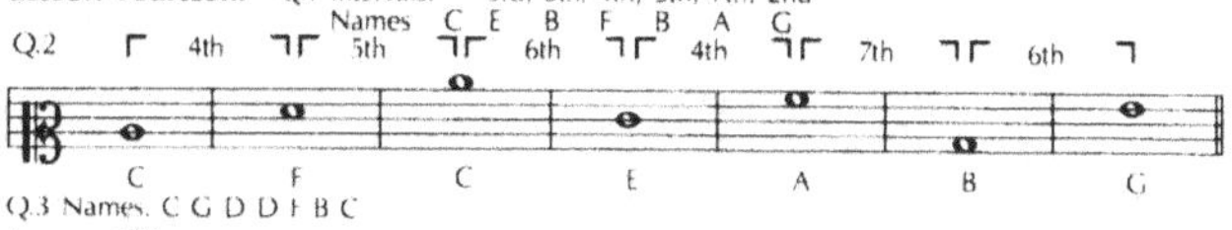

Q.3 Names: C G D D F B C C E A B G

Lesson Fifteen: 1. Grave 2. lively and fast 3. Ritardando, Rallentando 4. Prestissimo
5. return to the original speed 6. Andante 7. Allegretto 8. Accelerando

Q.1 **Lesson Seventeen:**

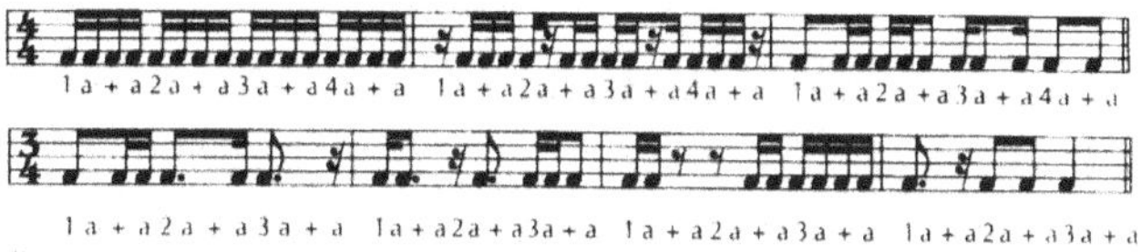

Q.2

Q.3 Other combinations of notes are possible for this question.

Q.4

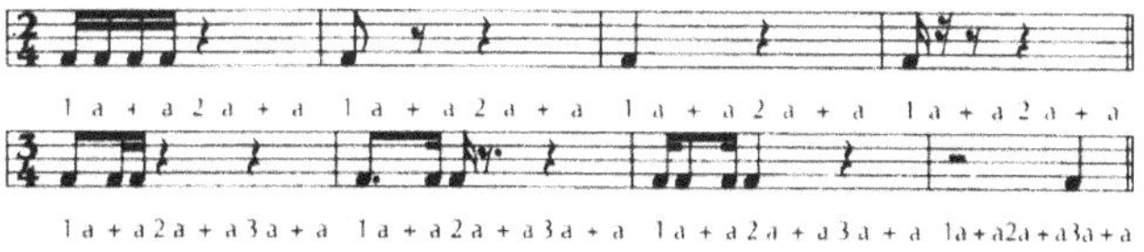

Lesson Eighteen:
Q.1 Q.2

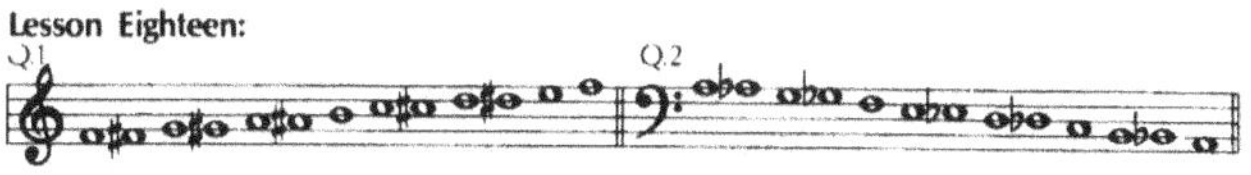

Lesson Twenty-One:
Q.1

ANSWER SHEET

Q.2

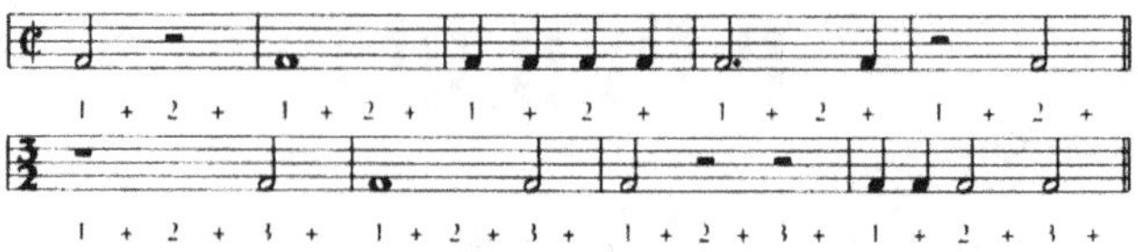

Q.3 Other combinations of notes and rests are possible.

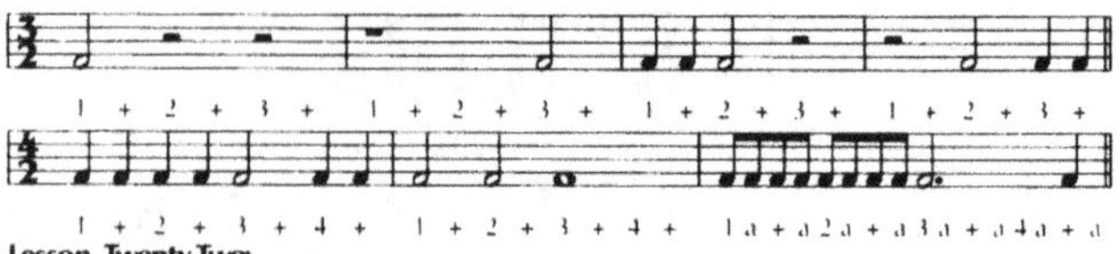

Lesson Twenty-Two:

Q.1

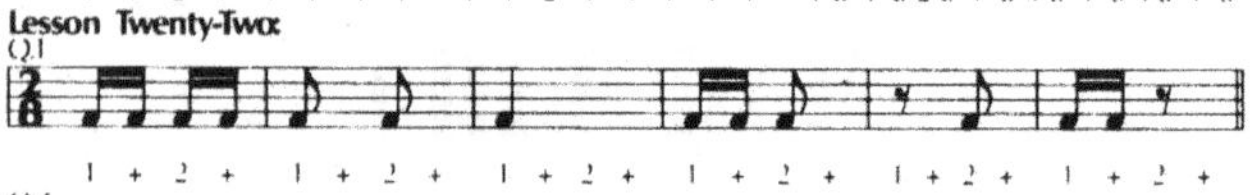

Q.2

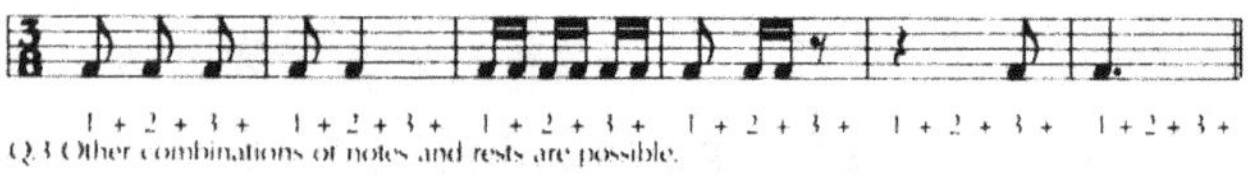

Q.3 Other combinations of notes and rests are possible.

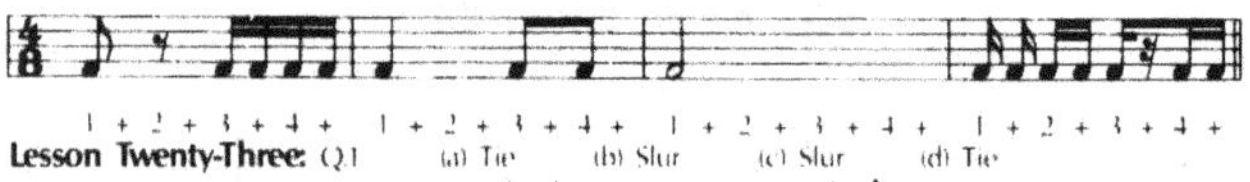

Lesson Twenty-Three: Q.1 (a) Tie (b) Slur (c) Slur (d) Tie

Q.2

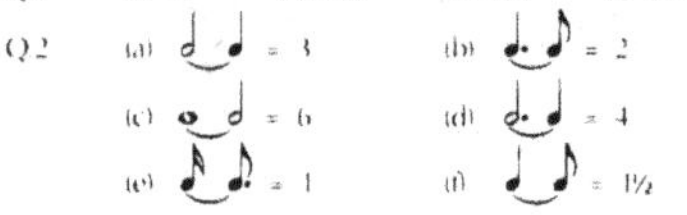

Lesson Twenty-Four: 1. Louder 2. longer 3. an octave higher 4. smoothly 5. detached 6. same 7. Loco

Lesson Twenty-Five: Maj3, m3, Maj3, Maj3, m3, m3, Maj3, m3

Q.1

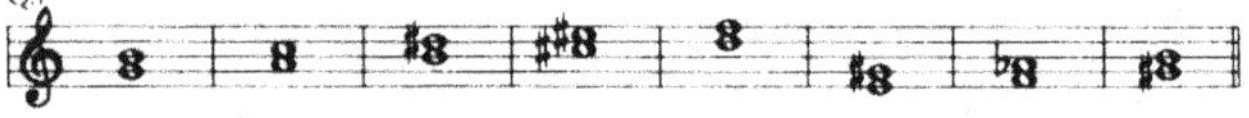

Lesson Twenty-Six:

Q.1

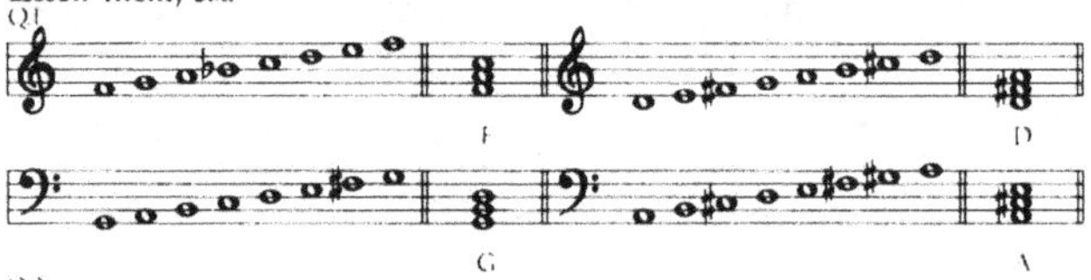

Q.2

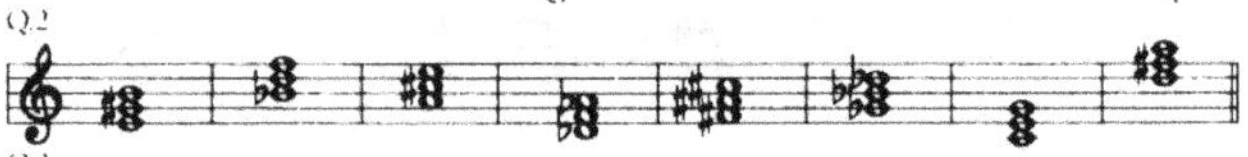

Q.3

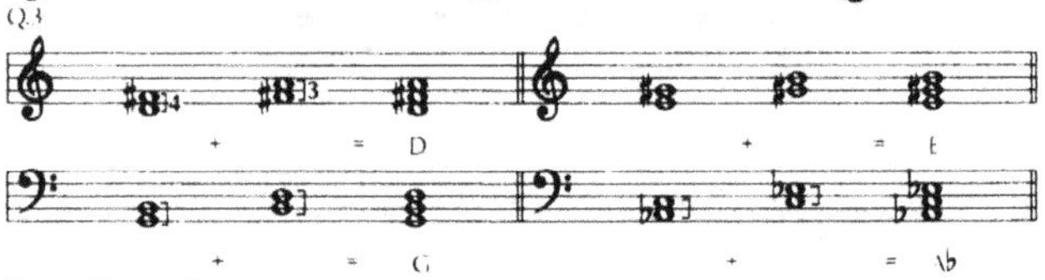

Lesson Twenty-Seven:

Q.1

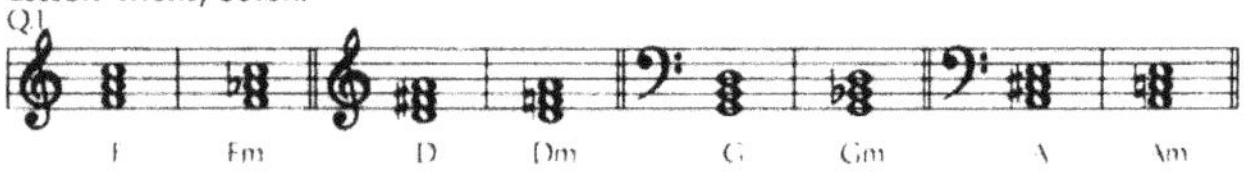

Q.2

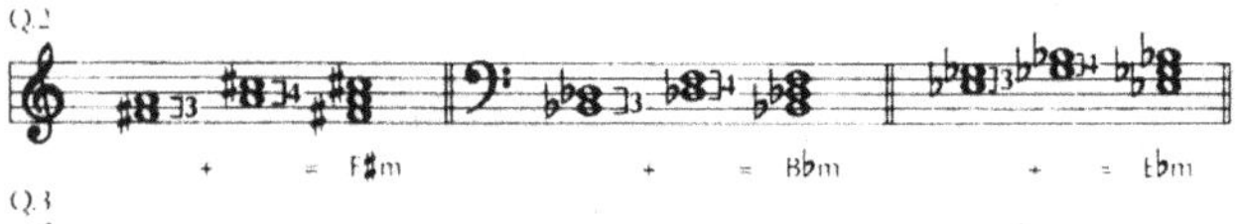

Q.3

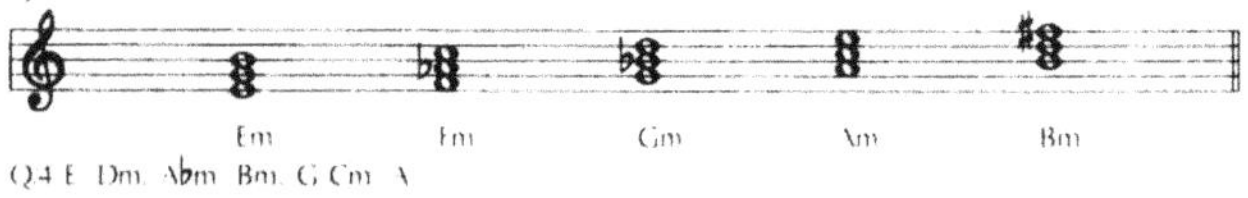

Q.4 E Dm Abm Bm G Cm A

Lesson Twenty-Eight:

Q.1

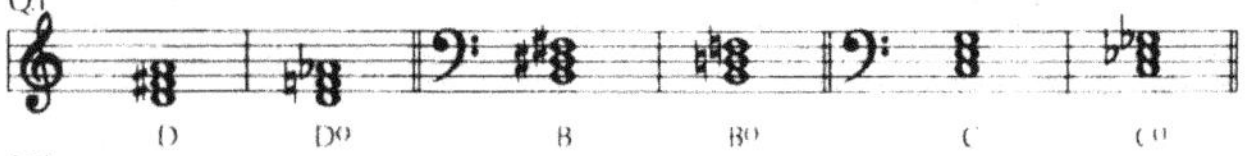

Q.2

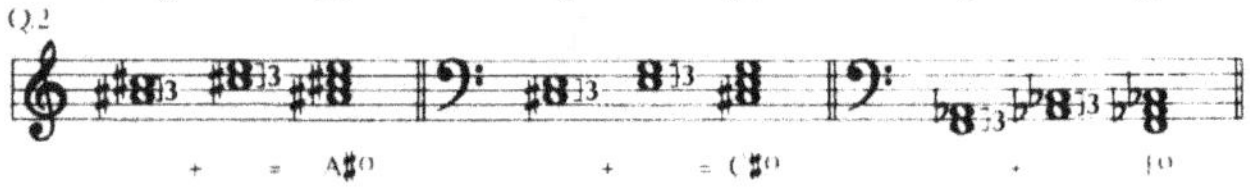

Q.3

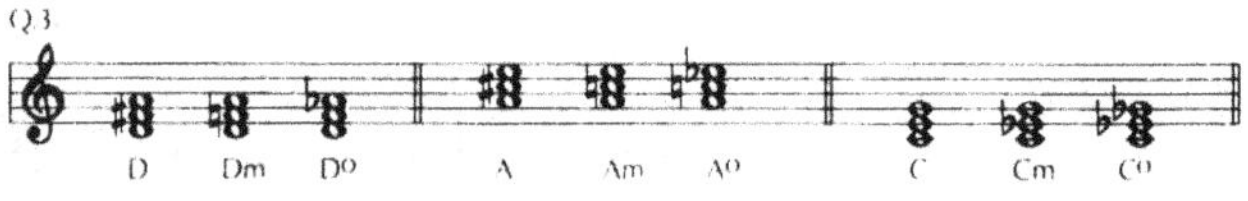

Lesson Twenty-Nine:

Q.1

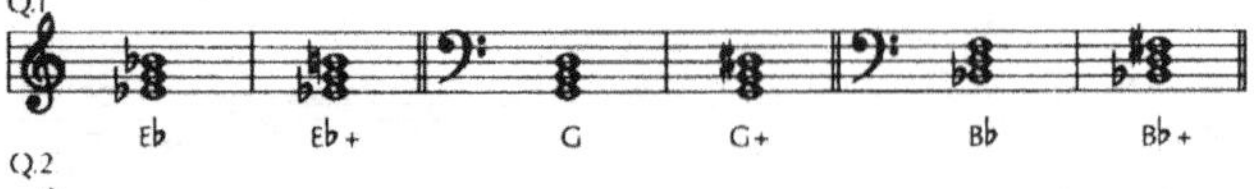

Q.2

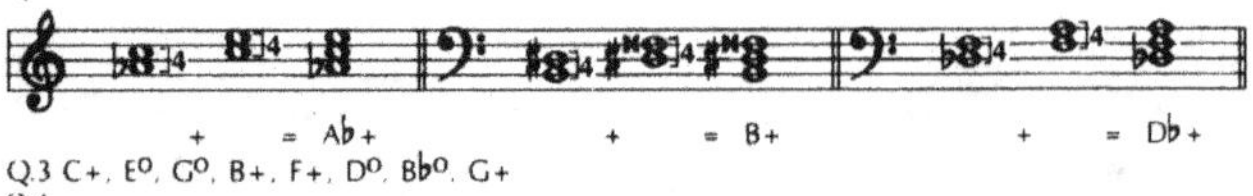

Q.3 C+, Eo, Go, B+, F+, Do, Bbo, G+

Q.4

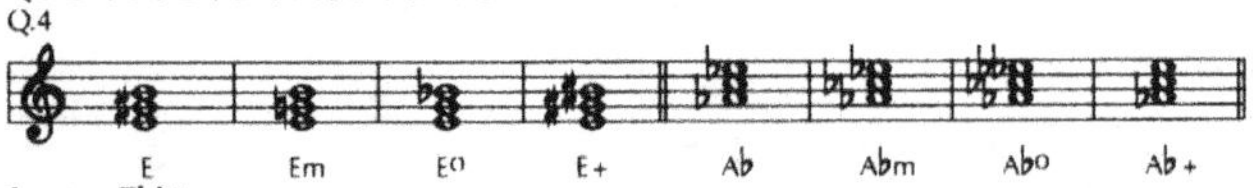

Lesson Thirty:

Q.1

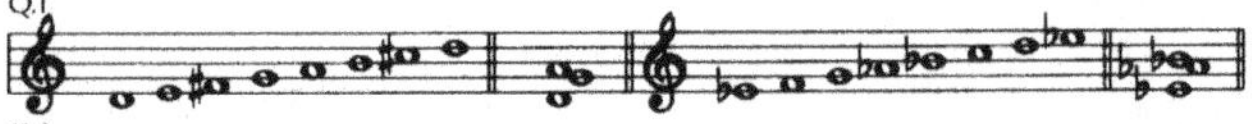

Q.2

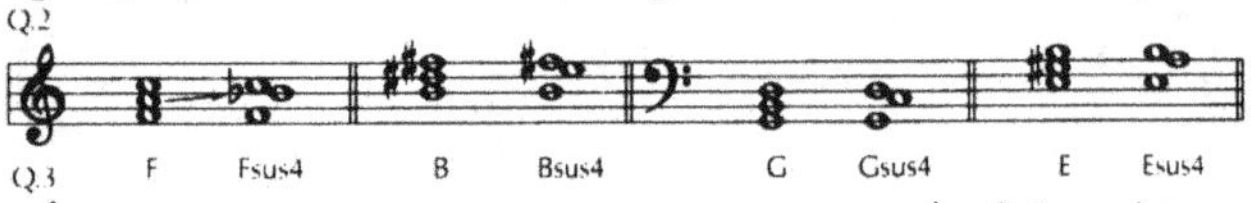

Q.3

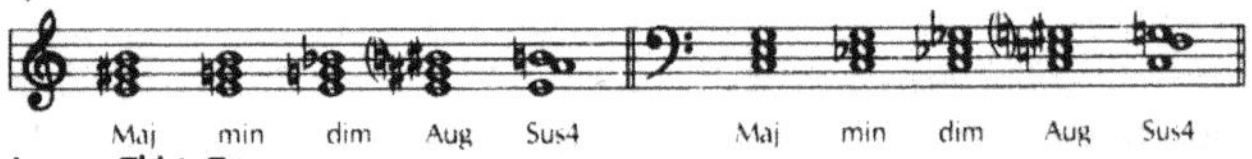

Lesson Thirty-Two:

Q.1

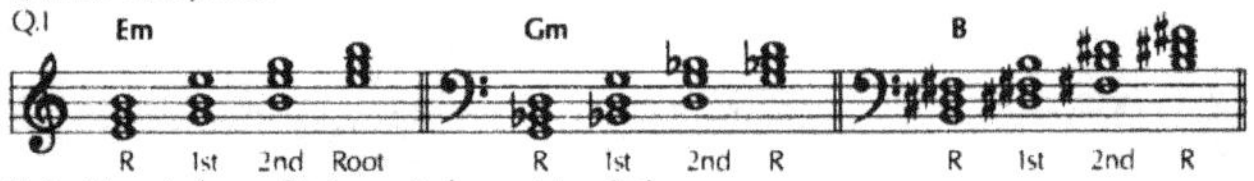

Q.2 1st 2nd Root 2nd 1st 2nd
Top Middle Bottom Middle Top Middle

Q.3

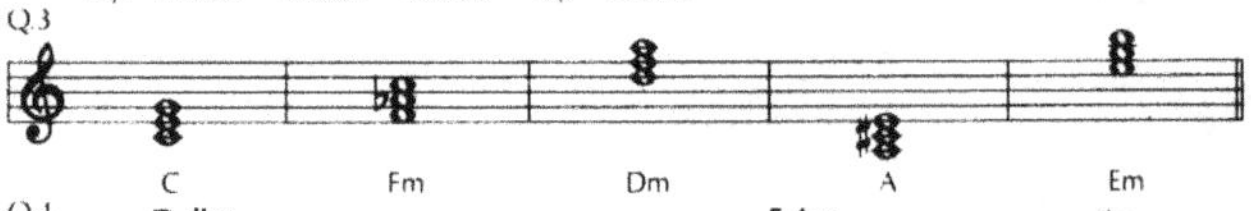

Q.4

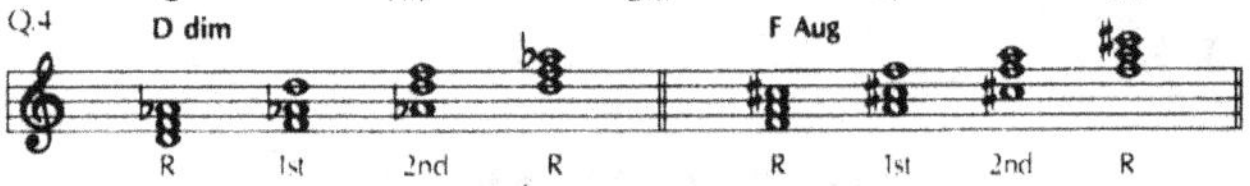

Q.5

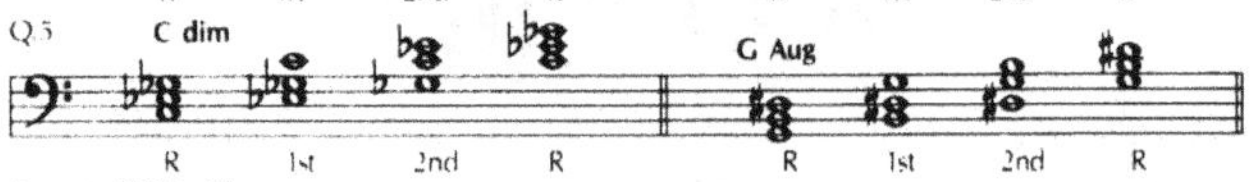

Lesson Thirty-Three:

Q.1

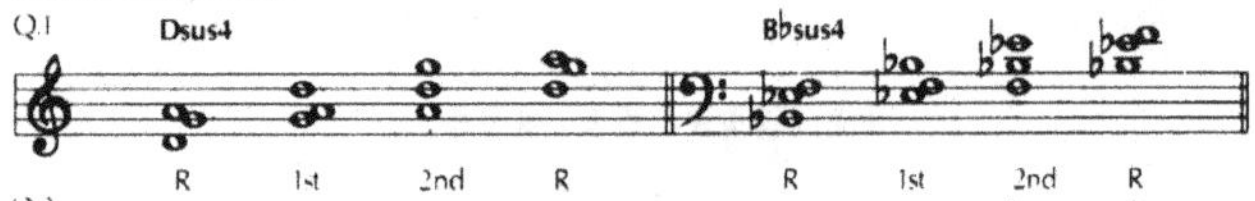

Q.2

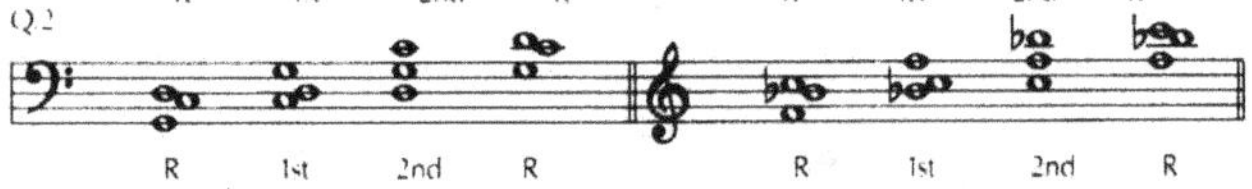

Q.3 Csus4 Eb Do Bmi G+
Q.4 C+ Ab Gsus4 Ami Bo
Q.5 Eo Bsus4 F+ F# Ebmi

Lesson Thirty-Five:

Q.1

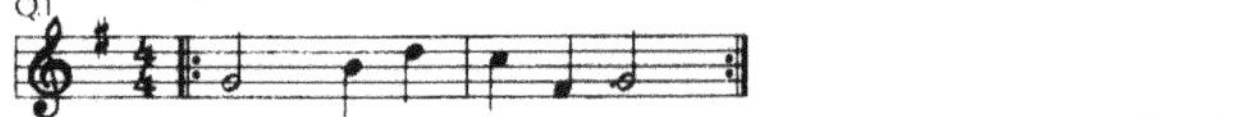

Q.2

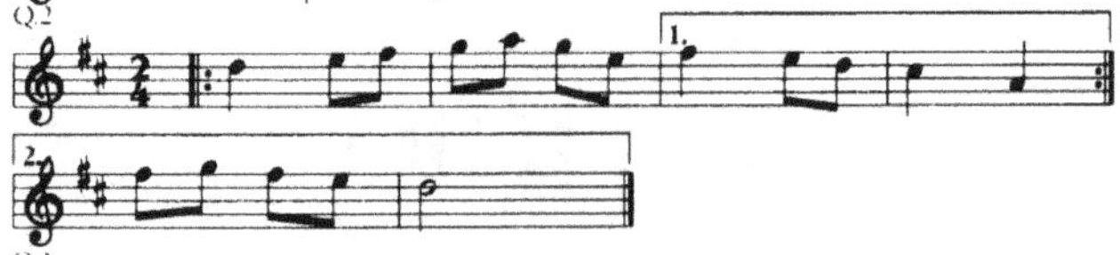

Q.3

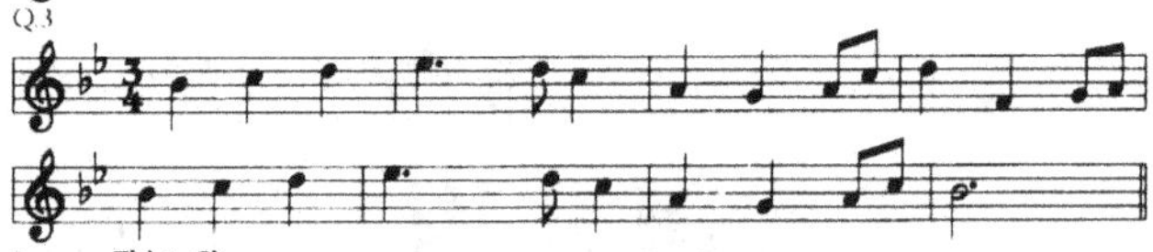

Lesson Thirty-Six:

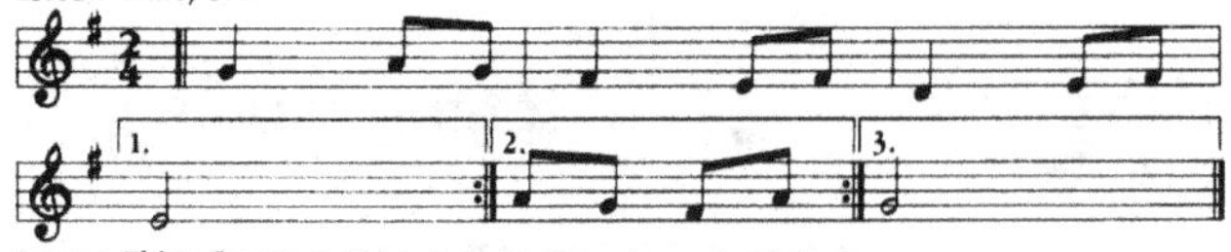

Lesson Thirty-Seven: 1. 6th 2. down 3. three 4. two 5. BEAD
6. 1st, 3rd, 5th or Tonic, Mediant, Dominant
7. FCGDAEB 8. very fast 9. Sixteen
10. 4 11. Diminished 12. Prime, 3rd, 5th and 7th
13. B Major 14. very loud 15. 3/2, 3/4, 3/8
16. make larger 17. Tonic and Dominant 18. Soprano
19. two 20. three flats, BEA 21. Cut Common Time or Alla Breve time
22. two tetrachords: whole tone, whole tone, half tone (Tone, Tone, Semitone)
23. Tie 24. detached, staccato
25. Major, Minor, Diminished, Augmented and Suspended Fourth

www.ingramcontent.com/pod-product-compliance
Lightning Source LLC
Chambersburg PA
CBHW081524160426
43195CB00015B/2479